Kids Mean Business

Kids Mean Business

How to Turn Your Love of Children
Into a Profitable
and Wonderfully Satisfying Business

Barbralu Manning

Live Oak Publications
Boulder, Colorado

Library of Congress Cataloging in Publication Data
Manning, Barbralu, 1949-
Kid's Mean Business

1. Infants' supplies industry. 2. Toy industry. 3. Children's clothing industry. 4. Play schools. 5. Day care centers. 6. New business enterprises. I. Title
HD9970.5.I542M36 1985 680 84-21830
ISBN 0-911781-03-X

The author and publisher have attempted to ensure the accuracy of all information in this book. Errors can occur, however, and requirements for starting a business are changed from time to time and can vary from place to place. For these reasons the publisher and author disclaim responsibility for the total accuracy of this book. Professional legal and accounting advice should be sought by anyone starting a business.

ISBN: 0-911781-03-X

Library of Congress Catalog Card Number: 84-21830

Published by Live Oak Publications
   6003 N. 51st Street
   P.O. Box 2193
   Boulder, CO 80306
   (303) 530-1087

Distributed by Liberty Publishing Company, Inc.
   50 Scott Adam Rd.
   Cockeysville, MD 21030
   (301) 667-6680

To my parents and to Nathan,
with my love and gratitude

Contents

Chapter 1
New Opportunities
In Kid-Related Businesses

A number of trends are at work today that are creating outstanding opportunities for starting your own kid-related business. If you love kids and want the unique independence and satisfaction of being your own boss, this is good news indeed.

In the pages that follow you'll find out exactly why the opportunities in this field are growing so fast today and how you can take advantage of the specific opportunities which appeal to you.

Self-employment means independence, self-fulfillment and the lack of a ceiling on your income, and in the field of children's products and services you can go just as far as your abilities will take you. Some people are tremendously successful:

- Joan Barnes was the new mother of a baby girl when she took a part-time job developing a play and exercise program for tots at her local community center. Based on the success of that class, a friend loaned her the money to buy mats and play equipment so she could start her own class in a rented space. Today about 15,000 preschoolers participate in classes across the country in Barnes' franchised Gymboree centers. Revenues are over a million dollars a year.

• When 32-year-old Tricia Fox and her husband couldn't find the type of day care they wanted for their three children, Tricia left her well established career selling computers and founded Fox Day Schools, Inc. After five years in business she operates six day care centers, plans to open five more in the near future, and is preparing to sell franchises in some 40 states.

• Pansy Ellen Essman was a 48-year-old factory worker when she got the idea for her business. It all began when she attempted to bathe her slippery, squirming first grandchild in a bathtub. That night she took her aching back to bed and had a dream about a urethane sponge bath aid that supports a baby in the tub, making the bath both safer and easier to give. Out of the dream was born Pansy Ellen Products, Inc., which has sold more than 10 million bath aids and last year grossed $5 million manufacturing products for infants and children.

• Kathy Kolbe got angry about the quality of education available for her gifted children in the Phoenix schools, and it was out of that anger that her business was born. Today, at 42, she heads five corporations dedicated to teaching children and adults the art of thinking, with sales projected at $3.5 million this year.

GOURMET BABIES: TRENDS BEHIND THE OPPORTUNITIES

There is nothing mysterious about the growth of products and services for children. A number of trends are at work contributing to the growth of this field.

The "Echo" Baby Boom

Look around in any American city today and you'll notice pregnant women with briefcases and graying parents pushing strollers. The post-World War II baby boomers, who were responsible for the biggest single population jump this country has ever seen, are now having babies of their own. This is the "echo" baby boom, and it has distinct characteristics which should be encouraging to anyone with an interest in kid-related self-employment.

Unlike previous generations, couples today are postponing having their families until they are well into adulthood. According to the Census Bureau, the number of women aged 30 to 34 having babies is increasing, while the number of 18- to 24-year-olds having children is declining. Because of this delay in having children, a much larger proportion of babies born today are first-borns. (In 1957 only about one fourth of the babies born in this country were firstborns; by 1980 that percentage had increased to almost one half.) Firstborns are, of course, more expensive to raise. They require the first crib, high chair, stroller, car seat, linens, clothes, toys, and sports equipment. They also inspire a flurry of grandparental spending. And as life spans continue to increase, so do the shopping days available to Grandma.

It will cost the average American family $226,000 to raise its firstborn son to the age of 22 and $247,000 for its firstborn daughter (blame such things as wedding expenses, cosmetics, and higher transportation costs for the difference), writes economist Lawrence Olson in his book, *Costs of Children.* That translates into more than $7.5 billion spent on child care and baby-sitting, $2.5 billion spent on clothing, $1.1 billion on preschool toys and more than $1 billion on cribs, playpens and car seats.

Growth of Two-Income Families

The development of this "echo" baby boom, with a greater proportion of firstborns, is clearly contributing to the growth in kid-related businesses. But perhaps even more important is the fact that the delay in having children today is directly related to Mom's decision to establish herself in a career before having a family.

The Census Bureau estimates that 50 percent of all

mothers of pre-schoolers work today. Two incomes mean more money for young parents to spend — and some stringent requirements on where it will be spent.

An executive in a large national department store chain, referring to these spending requirements, says: "Years ago, babies just wore the little stretchies for their first six months. Now Mom's going to work, so the child is going to a child care center or a baby-sitter. Little pajamas just won't do it."

As one working mother put it, "I don't have time to go shopping for bargains." She added, "Often times we come home at night and don't feel like making dinner, so we drag the kids out to eat. I just dress them up a lot because we're dressed up."

Besides, face it: Working moms feel guilty. After all, her mom was home, feeding her milk and cookies after school every day. Now she's toting around a briefcase while her child is being potty trained by someone else. Someone else is taking Junior to the pool for swimming lessons, to the zoo and to story hour at the library. To compensate, Mom is perfectly willing to spend her hard-earned money on classes, fancy educational aids and toys in the hope that somehow, even in her absence, she can stimulate her child's mind, promote his health and provide him with cuddles.

"The working mother feels guilty about not being home. She isn't there to teach her child every day, so she buys these educational toys," notes toy industry consultant Ruth B. Roufberg. One result is that developmental toy sales climbed nearly 50 percent in a recent two-year period, to about $150 million in sales.

Divorce Rates

High divorce rates also contribute to the growth of kid-related businesses. Although the divorce rate now seems to have leveled off, the overall number of divorces is expected to remain high. There's a growing trend toward joint custody arrangements, too, and increasingly Junior is shuttled between two homes. That often means two sets of beds, linens, teddy bears, story books and all the rest.

Increasing Quality

The statistics on delayed child rearing, two career families, increased educational toy sales and divorce rates can only reflect changes in quantity. While these trends are important, the changing *quality* of raising children today is equally important.

Not only are today's parents older, they are also better educated and more mature than previous generations of parents. And World War II baby boomers are ever upwardly mobile.

"These people attach everything with seriousness: their careers, their raising a child, the national debt," says a Cincinnati psychologist who runs an infant-toddler learning program.

"They approach parenting with the same energy, enthusiasm and excitement that they have given their personal lives and careers," notes a Washington pediatrician.

One new parent, an editor in South Carolina, says,

"I have learned that if you want something good, you go after it, whether it's a job or a promotion, or having the kind of kid you want."

For most baby-boomers, that means giving their children the advantages of anything that will create emotional security, self-confidence, physical fitness and a head start on education. Fitness centers now cater to tots from coast to coast. Infant stimulation, computer camps, foreign language classes, music, art and dance schools, flash cards, educational toys and cassette tapes proliferate as the demand for a quality childhood increases.

For many of today's young, urban professionals (the "Yuppies"), nothing is too good for baby. Mom, Dad, Grandma and Grandpa — to say nothing of Junior's still childless aunts and uncles — aren't just buying strollers and booties. They're indulging themselves as they indulge the child. They're equipping the nursery and they're clothing their little darlings in a way that reflects their own unbeatable sense of style, their own good taste.

They're buying blocks from the Museum of Modern Art for $25. Silk dresses for little girls imported from Italy for $120. Tyrolean-motif lederhosen for $33. Embroidered christening gowns for $175. Handcrafted cradles for up to $300 and Silver Cross English prams for $573.

Today there is a wider array of child-related merchandise than ever before. Style has become critically important. Nursery-accessory producers now change their lines with the seasons to keep up with changing fashion trends.

The designer nursery is in. Cloth sculptures, custom-built cabinets and changing tables, handmade crafts on the shelves and hanging from the ceiling are creating the "environment where children can grow and explore," as one designer phrased it. It's not just "the kids' room" any more.

Names like Calvin Klein, Christian Dior, Florence Eiseman — in silks, laces, velvets and denims — are turning up on everything from sleepers and diapers to tiny suits and gowns. The Izod alligator is crawling through nurseries all over America. Scaled-down versions of the latest adult clothing styles are rapidly gaining in popularity.

Not all of the increased spending is frivolous, of course. Busy mothers need front packs and back packs, baby carriers and bicycle seats to free up their hands. Car seats are considered essential, even mandatory as more and more states legislate safety restraints for children.

Quality is sought even in the bare necessities of kids' gear. An Anaheim mother bought a stroller for $185 because "it looks so racy" and folds up conveniently for trips like the one the family took to Hawaii. "You can get a stroller for $50, but I think you look for quality and appearance. You find something that's going to fit into your lifestyle," she explained.

SEIZING THE OPPORTUNITIES

For all the above reasons, the juvenile market is expanding. Even during the recent recession, juvenile product sales (excluding toys and clothes) grew at least 14 percent a year, according to the Juvenile Products Manufacturers' Association.

Self-employment in this field, as in any other, requires a total commitment and plain hard work. The demand for children's products and services is steadily growing, however, and this is one field where, with enough determination and energy, you can reach the goal of being your own boss.

"You know what I'd tell someone who wants to go into business for himself? Don't do it," says Dale Prohaska with a big laugh. He's joking, but maybe only half joking. The founder of Love-Built Toys and Crafts, Inc. of Tahoe City, California, was teaching school eight years ago when he started his business with an investment of $55. Last year he broke half a million dollars in sales.

"At this point it would be very difficult to work for somebody else," reflects Prohaska. "If I had to, I suppose I could."

But being in business for yourself is not always easy either, he continues. "You have to know yourself, what you like and don't like, what your personality is like. What's the old saying? You have to be a 'jack-of-all-trades, master of none.' You have to do it all — accounting, typing, taxes, mailing, drafting, layout, order processing. If you don't want to do all the little jobs, you're doomed from the beginning."

It's a struggle, he says. But in the end he admits, "I don't want to do anything else."

Kathy Kolbe, whose business is now the world's largest publisher of educational aids for gifted students, recommends that people analyze their motivations before taking the self-employment route. If you want power, try politics. If you want prestige, become a professor. "But if you can't imagine not doing it, if it's something you truly believe in, go for it," she says. "You know you're the entrepreneurial type if you're always thinking of how to market, who to sell to, when to offer your idea. In spite of the negatives, if you're bursting with the desire to do it — do it."

After ten years of doors being closed, vendors missing deadlines, work being turned in that failed to meet her exacting standards, Kolbe says there's nothing in the world she'd rather be doing. "Day in and day out your neck is on the block. But there's nothing in the world more fun and gratifying professionally."

Babies and children — to say nothing of their parents and grandparents, the people you'll really be marketing to — are crying for new classes, clothes, books, furniture, toys, and all sorts of services. The market is there. The need is there. The rewards — both in terms of personal satisfaction and financial independence — are there. This book will help you to focus your ideas and channel them down the (occasionally rocky) road to success. The possibilities are limited only by your imagination.

Chapter 2
From Art to Zoology:
The Teaching Business

Most people who love kids would agree that there are few things as rewarding as teaching. Watching children learn and develop as a direct result of your efforts can be supremely satisfying and fulfilling.

The problem is that most of us associate teaching with salaried positions in public or private schools. Teaching jobs are notoriously low paid, they often involve working in stifling bureaucracies, and some public schools essentially warehouse children with little effort to provide a creative learning environment.

TEACHING AS SELF-EMPLOYMENT

The alternative, of course, is to go into the teaching business on your own. But is this a realistic option?

To a surprising degree, the answer is yes. According to the Small Business Administration, in recent years "educational services" was the one category accounting for the largest number of new businesses. And the segment of educational services consisting of companies with fewer than 100 employees has grown as much as 26 percent annually.

It's not hard to understand the growing demand responsible for all those new education businesses. Today's baby-boom parents want their kids to succeed. Just as *they* strive to be physically fit, financially successful, mentally active and emotionally balanced — they feel that education is the key to similar achievements for their children.

Today's parents want their kids to move with grace, to master computers, to express themselves artistically, to appreciate nature, to handle hammers and saucepans with equal ease, and to be socially adept.

Read any of the new parenting books on the market and you'll find the same message: Children need to sample all different kinds of activities to discover their own unique talents. Experiencing a wide range of activities — from academics to arts and sports — teaches a child to concentrate, to observe, to see beauty in the world, to find answers to questions, and, as one book puts it, to "grow up with a zesty 'what's next?' view of life."

Because of this attitude, this idea that a wide variety of educational experiences can contribute to a well rounded, successful youngster — the market for children's educational services is booming today. There is a broad range of opportunities in tutoring, in starting your own school, and in teaching classes that you create yourself.

TUTORING

Without a doubt, tutoring is the simplest type of teaching business you can start. By spreading the word among parents, school teachers, and administrators that you're offering individual tutoring in specific subject areas, you should be able to make $10 to $20 an hour on a part-time basis. You're likely to find that the greatest demand occurs just after school ends in the early summer, and that there is not much business in the fall — at least not until the first report cards come out.

Although this type of informal tutoring can provide a nice supplementary income, there are obviously limitations on how much you can earn. At least one enterprising individual has come up with a way to go a step beyond this informal approach to tutoring.

Candace Sinclair gave up her job as a fourth grade teacher and, using one bedroom as her home office, created Learning Tree Tutors three years ago. By the second year Learning Tree was profitable, and now Candace has some 50 tutors working for her on a contract basis, according to *Sideline Business.*

Learning Tree essentially functions as a tutoring agency. Candace works some 12 to 22 hours a week making telephone contacts and scheduling appointments with parents. The ages of most of her clients range from the elementary level through high school, although there are also a few college students.

Learning Tree charges $12 for a typical one-hour session held at the student's home. The tutor receives $7.50 of that, and Candace keeps the rest. Tutors are often unemployed or retired, but they all have teaching credentials and classroom experience.

Candace advises that people thinking about starting a similar business survey school principals to determine the local need, participate in school/parent organizations to meet clients, and limit their services to a fairly small geographical area. She is now considering expanding her business by offering skill development programs to businesses.

STARTING YOUR OWN SCHOOL

For more than one teacher of children, one classroom has multiplied into many. It's sometimes a slow process, but profits grow, and it's often rewarding in other ways as well.

Janet McCabe, whose two swim schools enroll up to 400 students a day in the summer, says she hasn't gotten rich in her ten years in the business. However, she is now grossing $180,000 a year. And though she worked as a camp counselor since high school and began teaching swimming in college, she says that competence in the sport, while necessary, is not what makes a good teacher.

What does make a teacher are communication skills, a love of children, and an ability to deal effectively with them.

Now directing 26 other instructors and still teaching herself, McCabe provides her staff with training in communication, interpersonal relationships and technical knowledge about swimming instruction. The staff is trained in child development, how to talk to kids and how to respond to kids' emotional needs. All are currently involved in a major research project on the social, psychological, language and physical development of children. From the research they hope to better understand what their students of various ages are going through in class. At certain ages within the first year or so, for example, children are often very clingy to their mothers. If a swim teacher needs to hold a child for a minute during a mother-baby class, the separation can be traumatic, so the teacher needs to know what the baby's going through to help her and her mother feel comfortable in the water.

Learning to consult with professionals was an important step in the evolution of Janet's business. "I realized the importance of having an accountant and attorney when I needed advice," she says. She took classes to help with management and to learn business procedures.

In looking back the main thing she feels she did right was to "move slowly. . . . I haven't taken one step beyond what I could handle."

Joan Barnes has also been successful, though with a different type of school and on an altogether different scale. As a new mother, Barnes found disappointingly few creative outlets for her and her daughter. So, working as a part-time employee at a community center, she went to work developing a play and exercise program for infants and toddlers. Her first class was successful, and a friend at the center loaned her $4,000 to buy play equipment and mats so she could set up her own class.

Operating her business out of a garden shed in her back yard, Barnes began to expand. Her program, named "Gymboree," went from revenues of $88,000 in 1980 to $375,000 in 1982 (the year it began franchising) without spending a penny for advertising. With something like 200 Gymboree franchise centers now operating, revenues are over a million dollars a year.

Gymboree members are between three months and four years old, and must be accompanied to the 45-minute class by a parent. During the classes the children roll around on huge foam-rubber logs, romp on ladders, and whiz down tiny slides. All equipment is designed and made to Barnes' specifications.

Besides being fun, the classes help develop motor skills and invite active parental involvement. Barnes says that today's parents will pay just to spend time with their kids. She clearly believes she has tapped a new "child-service" industry.

ORGANIZING AND TEACHING CLASSES

Somewhere between informal tutoring and starting your own school is a third possibility — the opportunity to be self-employed as the teacher of a class you personally have designed and created.

What do you love to do? Whether you love to embroider shirts, watch birds, cook, dance, fix toaster ovens, or sing (even off-key) — all are experiences that can be shared with and explained to children. Do you like to make up stories? Go for walks in the woods? Those are the natural ingredients of children's activities,

activities that can be the gateway to broadening a child's world, engaging his imagination, and expanding his zest for living.

Maybe you're a college physics professor with an idea for starting a "Mr. Wizard"-style Saturday morning science class. Or you may be a retired grandpa who's been whittling as long as you can remember. Or a housewife who thinks that all you know how to do in the entire world is cook. No matter how you've acquired your particular skill, don't underestimate its value. If you're someone to whom other people turn for advice about a given subject, you've probably got the necessary background to develop your know-how into a course for kids.

If you're not quite confident (and what first-time teacher doesn't get nervous?) it may help to fortify your knowledge by reading books, talking to professionals in your field and talking to other teachers. You might arrange for one or two professionals to talk to your class. Having experienced teachers critique your course plan can reassure you that what you're planning to do is realistic.

When teaching kids, it's important not to talk down to them, and yet you must reach them at their own level. A five-year-old takes himself pretty seriously (except when he's joking). So does a three-year-old or a ten-year-old for that matter. Respect your students. As one teacher put it, "They're probably smarter than you anyway."

There is always the danger, of course, of assuming that your students know more about your particular subject than they really do. You must start with the basics to give them a good, solid foundation from which to build their own expertise, whether it concerns bird nesting habits, the proper procedure for glazing ceramics or how to approach a gymnastics mat. Along with the basics, you need to impart a respect for order, for proper procedure, for safety, for clean-up. Kids need to learn the value of putting things away so that they can be found next time, of following established procedures and of feeling good about a job well done. They need to learn to show respect for themselves and others by obeying safety rules and cleaning up work areas.

Requirements

To teach classes successfully there are several qualities you should possess:

- warmth and a sense of compassion for children
- expertise in your subject area (regardless of how you acquired it)
- patience
- genuine enthusiasm — both for your students and for your subject matter
- a sense of humor

It is also necessary to understand that kids have different learning styles. According to Grace Johnson, director of teachers at one of the largest alternative education institutions in the U.S., 40 percent of children learn visually, 40 percent learn through hands-on experience and only 20 percent grasp information and concepts auditorily. "So if you lecture all the time, you've lost 80 percent of them."

To get through to all the ways kids take in what they're learning, try a variety of different techniques. Along with lecturing, use films, slides, demonstrations, and small group work, and always allow plenty of time for practice.

Planning can make the difference between a class which never really "gels" and a class that is clearly successful. The tool which makes the difference is the course plan worksheet, detailing the content of the course, the process that will be used to present that content and your expectations about what the students will gain from the course. Such a worksheet will prompt you to think about what you're going to do and how you're going to do it — to set meaningful goals and determine how to reach those goals.

The Question of Discipline

Unfortunately, discipline is an issue you'll need to think about if you're considering teaching kids for the first time. Talk to other teachers and read books on the subject. Think about how you most effectively work as an authoritative, yet loving parent, or talk to parents who have a way with their kids that you admire. From wiggly, squirming preschoolers to adolescents who think they'd rather be elsewhere, you need to establish respect from Day One. You need to start out in a firm environment so the kids understand that you are the teacher and what you say, goes. Then you can move into a friendly, warm relationship with each child. As Grace Johnson put it, "When kids understand that you're the authority and that they're there to learn, they have fun, they learn, and your problems are reduced."

A Survey of Possibilities

This list is intended to stimulate your imagination and is by no means comprehensive. If you already know what you want to teach, great. If not, begin by considering those pastimes you most enjoy. Your personal enthusiasm is absolutely essential to your success.

Survey what's currently available in your city. Ask the owners of toy stores and day-care centers what classes are available — and what aren't. Check with your public school district's continuing education division, nearby colleges, your city recreation department, state and national park offices, YMCA or YWCA, planetarium, and museums to see what they offer for kids. All these places are also potential sponsors of your class.

Science

As any parent will tell you, children from the earliest age examine their surrounding environment with great interest and care. A child's search for similarities and differences — between boys and girls, between rubber balls and pie tins, between dogs and bicycles — is the foundation for all their future knowledge. A child observes, experiments, experiences — and isn't that the heart of science? Children begin life as scientists, testing their world, making hypotheses, gathering data, building conclusions and new hypotheses.

There are few limits to a child's curiosity, and if presented at a level a child can understand, classes in areas as diverse as biology, geology, field ecology, chemistry, archaeology, astronomy, dinosaurs, the human body, sensory awareness — all can be successful.

Visual Art

Whether a child weaves a potholder or sculpts a duplicate of The Pieta, whether he scribbles or draws with unmistakable talent, learning about art is learning about creativity. It's a connection in the most direct way with the physical and spiritual forces that shape us and our world. Lucky is the child who is guided in those experiences, and lucky is the teacher who can awaken a true appreciation for art.

Perhaps above all else, the role of the art teacher is to provide encouragement. The amount of supervision needed varies according to the specific project and the age of the children, but essentially it is the teacher's job to simply explain the technique, help the students as they work and then help them clean up.

Providing an environment that allows freedom for creativity, without the fear of failure, is essential. As teacher Ellen Press Mendelsson puts it: "The child who has been made overanxious by too high standards, by working only with coloring books, number painting sets or copying patterns, finds it increasingly difficult to express his own views in any art medium. Perhaps our most important role in a child's artistic development is to allow the free exploration of materials.''

A patient teacher, in other words, will encourage a young child who is more enthralled with a blob of paint gushing through his fingers than with producing a recognizable painting of a cat.

It *is* a mess. But some people have found a way to turn even that problem into an opportunity. Ellen Hall and Debbie D'Allessandro teach a course called ''Making a Mess'' through their local community schools program. Finger painting with chocolate pudding, sitting in a sandbox filled with puffed oats, throwing balloons at each other — one- and two-year-olds love the course, which permits more freedom than even the most lenient parent is likely to allow.

''Most mothers say they would love to do this at home, but they don't want to clean up the mess,'' says D'Alessandro.

Choice of Media

By two years of age, most kids are competent with stick figure drawings. A three-year-old can draw circles, lines and dots at will. The older a child gets, though, the more limited his drawings tend to become in size and fluidity — unless he's guided to draw by the imaginative teacher who takes him outside to draw in the air with his arms.

Most art teachers think that pens and pencils are

too limiting for many purposes. Jumbo crayons are enthusiastically grabbed by one- and two-year-olds. By two, kids love chalk, which blends and smears to their hearts' delight. By six a child can handle pastels, the more sophisticated relative of chalk. All children seem to love felt markers, but close supervision will be needed if you're concerned about the looks of your classroom walls.

Batik (with you manning the iron), block printing, pasting, cutting, collage, transfers, and wax papered window pictures are also a hit with young children. Every age loves to paint. Finger paints and poster paints are most commonly recommended for younger children; oils take too long to dry, watercolors require too much delicacy, and acrylics may be too thick to be applied easily to paper.

Use your imagination in coming up with other media. Even a two-year-old can know the joy of working with clay, although throwing on a wheel isn't appropriate until much older. And if the clay can be dug during an expedition to a nearby park or stream bed, so much the better.

Crafts

Author and children's editor Seymour V. Reit says that making things with kids requires only "a sense of fun, some imagination and a willingness to explore and experiment." If you want to teach but aren't 100 percent confident, "don't fret," he says. "Children — especially the younger ones — are not perfectionists;

they don't expect precise works of art. All they want to do is have a good time — and so should you.''

Yet there are guidelines to follow. One is determined by the age of the child. If he attempts to make something that's too difficult, he will become frustrated; if it's too easy, he'll become bored. In either case, he's likely to lose interest in his creative abilities.

Crafts seems to grow in value as our society becomes more mechanized and materialistic. As Reit said, ''Today's children are growing up in a rapid action world dominated by a kind of fast-food mentality, an environment that is built around instant gratification. Almost everything in modern society comes ready-made — everything except sensitivity, growth and learning. For this reason a balancing influence is needed — something that will help kids to learn patience and to develop their personal creative skills. Children need help in gaining the ability to create things of their own which, if not 'instant,' can provide gratification of a richer and deeper kind.''

Imagine a child's pride at bringing home a potholder or a primitive spoon rest that actually gets used — much less an embroidered picture that gets framed and hung. Dolls, masks, dried and pressed or arranged flowers, woven rugs or hangings, beanbags or other toys, embroidered aprons or pictures, handmade books — whatever crafts a child brings home, she brings with pride. She's mastered a skill. She's blended colors and textures and whipped them into shape with scissors or a simple loom. She's given birth to something that didn't exist before she created it. And, it's been fun.

Drama

"The child with a dramatic imagination has 100 playmates and 1000 games," wrote two mothers. At first, teaching dramatics may be as simple as providing a story hour where you help children act out their favorite stories or have them make up their own stories, each in his or her own turn. Later they pretend with costumes and learn to assume new personalities both because it broadens their understanding of people and because it's fun. Finally, they'll advance to puppets, old-fashioned theatricals and fully staged productions.

Dance

From the moment he can pull himself up to standing, a baby dances to his own rhythm. We are all dancers, and children can be taught to recognize that dance is as natural as any other kind of movement. Dance can also help children counteract the bad posture and clumsiness which sometimes moves over them as they grow.

Marguerite Kelly and Elia Parsons, who wrote *The Mother's Almanac*, beautifully defined the role of the dance teacher: "A good teacher extracts individual expression, giving only enough direction to create the order the children need to respond to the music as well as to each other. Judge the teacher's ability by the grace and ease of her body, the warmth and encouragement she shows and how well she understands how they're built so that none of the movements she suggests will strain their muscles — the most critical knowledge she can have."

Across the country "creative movement" classes are introducing kids from toddlers on up the fun of movement and the possibilities of their own bodies. Some are combined with an introduction to sound, incorporating rhythm and music preparatory instruction. The Hebrew Arts School in New York City includes modern, folk and ballet classes taught by former American Ballet Theatre principals. You may not have that kind of background, but if you love kids and love to dance and feel competent to teach dance, that's enough to get you going.

Music

In more and more cities a kind of music-appreciation-for-tots movement is springing up. The well known Carl Orff and Suzuki group teaching methods have been a major stimulus to the realization that kids as young as two can play and appreciate music.

Early music classes teach kids to listen, hear and express. Singing is always popular with kids, especially songs with animal sounds, with finger play, with lots of repetition and silly or funny lyrics. As children grow, they begin to enjoy songs in which all the lines are echoed, songs that allow them to make up rhymes, songs in which words are added with each verse, action songs, rounds or partner songs and folk songs. Along with singing, early music classes may include some primitive instrumentation — pounding on a drum, jingling keys, scraping teeth of a comb, playing kazoos.

Most experts agree that standard, individual lessons

are not appropriate for the very young child, but for older children, traditional music lessons are experiencing renewed popularity.

Language

Classes are springing up across the country to teach conversational French, Spanish, Italian — even Chinese — to children from age four and up, and in many areas there's a need for immigrants to learn English as a second language as well. Parents know that there's no better time for learning a second language than the early childhood years.

Computer Skills

"Computer literacy" has become a catch phrase of the '80s, and many parents are concerned that their own lack of familiarity with computers could handicap their children. As computer hardware and software continue to become more "user friendly," this concern may lessen, but for the moment there is a solid market for classes which introduce kids to the basics of computers. Even as young as four, a child can learn to feel comfortable around a keyboard and video display, and have fun doing it. For older kids, simple programming courses are popular.

Cooking

Marguerite Kelly and Elia Parsons agree that instruction in basic cooking skills is fundamental and should be made available to all children. As they write in their wonderful book, *The Mothers' Almanac*: "We believe a child can gain more self-esteem in a kitchen than anywhere else, for to him, cooking probably is the most important job in the world."

Teach a child to cook and you teach him to follow instructions, to calculate, and to create. His sensory awareness is heightened by learning what tastes good with what, by inhaling the irrestible aroma of his own fresh-baked bread, and by judging the texture and consistency of dough. His arithmetic is honed by doubling recipes and learning equivalent units of measurement. He witnesses the miraculous transformation of goopy eggwhites into majestic meringues, and soupy cake batter into glorious desserts.

Safety rules must be established first thing — and strictly adhered to. For your peace of mind, avoid anything made with hot grease or boiling syrups. Use wooden utensils for stirring since they don't transfer heat. Keep all pot handles at the back of the stove so they can't be knocked over. Make sure aprons are worn and hands are washed before starting. Classes should be kept small so you can keep your eyes on everyone.

Cooking classes are fun for even the youngest children — who can help with measuring, stirring and beating. Let them mix things with their hands now and then, just because it's so messy and fun.

Then, of course, sit down together and enjoy the creations you've cooked up. If you save some for Mom and Dad, it can be a real plus for your on-going public relations effort.

Nature

Even in the middle of the city it's possible to inspire children's natural sense of awe at this magical world we live in.

Nobody's been around a four-year-old for more than five minutes without having to answer something along the lines of "How did they get the moon and stars up in the sky?" or "Why does the moon come out at night?" A good teacher will build on this curiosity and focus it so that the child begins to enjoy and love his natural surroundings.

You don't need a nature preserve to do that. Take a walk with your students around the block, focusing on what's under your feet. Or take the same walk blindfolded and smell and hear what's going on around you. Have them keep a seasonal diary of a small area, a park or their own back yard, perhaps. Teach them to use nature guides and go for a birding walk. Visit a planetarium and have a nighttime excursion into the heavens with the help of a sky chart. Plant a garden and watch it grow, or at least grow some vegetables and flowers indoors in containers.

GETTING STARTED

Along with deciding what you're going to teach and preparing a course plan worksheet, you'll need to put some thought into the nuts and bolts of your teaching business.

What to Charge

Just as any other business person does, you need to sit down and figure up all your expenses so that you'll know what kind of income you'll need to make a profit. This may be a good time to sit down with an accountant, just for one session, so he or she can help you determine your fees (and also fill you in on what records you're going to need to keep for the Internal Revenue Service). Your fees will have to cover all your expenses, including rent, utilities, supplies — and your salary.

To a large extent, what you can charge depends on your teaching qualifications and the level of demand in your area for the type of classes you offer. Check with other local schools and teachers to find out what they're charging. You want to be competitive, but if you're offering privately what the local recreation department offers only for groups, or if your program is unique and in great demand, your fees can reflect that by being a little higher than the average.

Music classes, for example, vary from $9 a half hour to $45 — and more — for instructors with outstanding reputations. Swim classes can range from about $10 to $20 per hour and can be quite a bit more in big cities. Group lessons, on the other hand, can be much lower.

While you're establishing your fees, you might want to establish some policies as well: When do you expect payment? If you want payment in advance, will you give refunds for any reason? What if students need to miss a lesson? Do they get to make it up? Do you charge them for it? Do you want a commitment for, say, six weeks — or six months? What if you're sick or need to miss a lesson?

It may seem a little overwhelming, but if you can plan for these things in advance — and maybe hand out copies of your policies when students register for your class — you can avoid most of the problems inherent in the teaching business.

Marketing

How do you find your students? Marie Blaney, who taught privately and at the University of Cincinnati College Conservatory of Music before opening her own school for children, says that "Getting the word out is really not hard, because parents tell other parents. Word of mouth is really your best bet."

In the beginning, though, you may want to distribute fliers around town or invest in some newspaper advertising. Chances are you'll start out small, as Blaney and Janet McCabe did, even if you go on to open your own school, too.

"Probably the best way to get people to enroll is to offer one free lesson," McCabe suggests.

If you decide to offer a free class, make sure you emphasize the benefit to your prospective students and their parents in your advertising (whatever type you use). A free lesson can give the child an opportunity to test his or her interest in the subject, without a long-term commitment or investment. Keep in mind, though, McCabe's experience: "Once you've got them there, if you're good, they'll stay."

You may decide to associate your class with the

local university or public school division of continuing education, your city's recreation department, a health club, art organization or art center, zoo, church, "Y" or other organization. If such a group sponsors you, they may help publicize your class and provide the space for your class to meet. In return they'll probably take a percentage of your earnings, however.

Whether you decide to teach totally on your own, out of your home or in rented space — or seek the sponsorship of an established group — the range of possibilities for teaching classes is almost endless. Parents understand the importance of exposing their kids to a broad spectrum of educational opportunities, and if you've got the enthusiasm and desire, there's probably something you could develop into a successful, popular — and potentially lucrative — course.

Chapter 3
Creative Child Care

The eighteen enrollment spots in the new child-care center in downtown Pittsburgh filled up overnight — and the center continued to receive up to sixty calls a week from parents wanting to place their kids. San Francisco's Pacific Heights Children's Center has a waiting list of up to three or four months. And La Petite Academy in Atlanta opened and filled eight centers in its first year of operation.

It would be hard to find a business with a more favorable economic outlook than child care. In 1965 less than 4 million children under six had working mothers. By 1980, that number had almost doubled, and by 1990 it is expected to exceed 10.5 million.

During your first year in business as a day care provider you can expect your earnings to be equivalent to the beginning salaries of professionals like designers, college teachers and social workers. If you work out of your home you should end up with more earned income after taxes, though, because of tax deductions you can take and expenses you won't be bothered with — transportation to and from work, parking, lunches away from home, clothing bought specifically for work and child care for your own children.

Day care can be a lucrative enterprise. And just as important are the intangible rewards of molding young children, pushing them along their paths toward self-confidence, discovery, social interaction, self-expression and creativity.

For women, especially, a day-care business is a solution to an increasingly common dilemma: You want to be with your children, but you need to contribute to your family's income.

It's not for everyone, of course. Home day care can mean long hours, evenings spent cleaning up and preparing for tomorrow, days spent almost entirely without adult company, disruption of your home and a major drain on the time and energy you can devote to yourself and your family.

But if you love children, perhaps have some little ones of your own, and are motivated to work and reap the financial rewards, child care may well fit your needs and be a rewarding way for you to reach your goals.

CHILD CARE DEFINED

Some definitions are in order because child care is a broad field and there are a number of different services you can provide for a variety of clients.

Day-care Homes

Day-care homes provide regular, less-than-24-hour care for children under the age of six. They ordinarily care for more than three children and are required to meet minimum health, safety and legal requirements. Most are open from about 7 a.m. to 6 p.m. to accommodate working parents, although some provide overnight or weekend care.

Day-care Centers

Day-care centers are the same as day-care homes except that they are usually larger and are not operated out of a home. The legal and licensing requirements for these facilities are often more stringent than those for day-care homes.

Drop-in Day Care

Emergency or drop-in care programs meet the spur-of-the-moment needs of parents. Drop-in care may be offered in addition to the regular services of a day-care home or center.

Before- and After-school Care

Day-care centers, homes and private and public schools may offer supervised care before and after school. Hours are usually from about 7 to 8 a.m. and again from about 3:30 to 6 p.m.

Nannies

A nanny goes to the child's home on a full-day, part-day, or live-in basis. Some live almost like family members, even traveling with the family on vacations. Most charge either hourly or daily rates and many do housework as well as child care.

REQUIREMENTS AND RESOURCES

According to Karen Thorensen, director of the Boulder, Colorado Child Care Support Center, a good day-care provider:

- wants to spend time with children

- has some background in childhood development — anything from the practical experience of raising her own family, to child development courses, to a degree in elementary education

- has the emotions behind the skills that Thorensen calls "the warmth factor"

- has the proper physical set-up in her home (for home day care)

Experts agree that, while a degree in childhood development could be helpful, it is less important than the motivation to give kids a loving environment in which to grow and flourish. No one who's ever raised children thinks being a good parent is totally instinctive, though. Resources in your community can provide you with the background and practical skills to help get you started:

• About a dozen child-care support centers across the country train providers and supply information about child-care resources. They may have literature to give or lend to you, classes on special care and on setting up your business, equipment to lend, technical assistance and referrals to new clients.

• If you don't have a support center in your area, contact your city or county social services department. Its personnel can tell you about licensing requirements and their procedure for making referrals, and they may be able to give you the same kind of assistance provided by child-care support centers in other areas.

• Read everything you can get your hands on (or have time for, whichever comes first) about early childhood development.

• Check out the programs available through your local community college, public school's division of continuing education or free school — even Lamaze or new parenting classes can be helpful. You'll learn what the norms are for every childhood age, what kind of behavior you can expect

and how to foster the optimum development of
your charges.

- Find out if there is a local organization of day-
care providers — or start one yourself. As with
any profession, the more you communicate with
your peers, the more you'll learn about doing the
job right. Getting together with other providers
can also help you to feel less isolated and give you
good ideas for dealing with the business side of
your operation.

- Take a course in first aid and cardiopulmonary
resuscitation (CPR). Prospective clients will ask
what kind of first aid training you have, so be
prepared.

- Talk to parents, librarians and teachers about
what kind of child care is most needed in your
community. Ask them for their ideas about what
makes a high quality child-care facility.

EXPANDING YOUR FAMILY

Starting any business in your home affects your
family to a degree, but a home day-care business can be
a bigger disruption than most. If your own children are
pre-school age or younger, your business may fit snugly
into their lives and your existing schedule. But if you
don't have kids, or if your kids are older, you need to sit
down with your family and discuss their needs, your

needs and the needs of your clients.

For up to twelve hours a day, at least five days a week almost year around, the tramp of little feet — and other sounds as well — will be heard in your house. Do your small children understand that they have to share their toys? Do your big kids understand that you just may not have the energy to cook full-course dinners every night? How does your spouse feel about having a significant amount of space in your home decorated with the alphabet and big-eyed stuffed animals? Is your family willing to help with housework, cooking, laundry and shopping? Even though you'll be at home, you'll be entering the work force. You may be able to get some housework done during the hours you're with your charges, but you just can't count on it.

"I couldn't do this without a supportive husband," says Tina Pyzik, who operates a day-care home named Greentree. Without children of their own, Tina and Chris, her architect husband, have built an impressive playground for her "school" of eight.

"Taking care of eight kids a day is not a nine-to-five job," she notes in what may be a mild understatement. Evenings usually find her cleaning up from the day, preparing for tomorrow's activities and meals. Weekends bring yard maintenance, equipment upkeep, and more cooking and grocery shopping for the week.

Tina has taken one sick day in two years of operation and about three weeks of vacation a year — two weeks at Christmas and a week in the summer. In addition, she closes on legal holidays like Memorial Day, Thanksgiving and Labor Day.

That doesn't leave a lot of time for her to lavish on herself or her spouse, which is what Karen Thorensen is referring to when she says "You need to look at your own mental health before you open a business like this. The only way you can be a good care provider is if you take care of yourself." Not only does the work require long hours, "it can drive you nuts not to talk to another adult day in and day out," she says.

The solution is to create time for yourself in the evenings or on weekends, or when you can afford it, to hire a substitute to give yourself a day off once in a while.

NUTS, BOLTS, AND OTHER CONSIDERATIONS

Licensing

Okay. You're still determined that child care is the opportunity for you. What do you do first?

The very first step is to contact the authorities where you live to see what your physical requirements will be. Most social service departments require fencing outside, a certain square footage per child inside, and basic safety precautions like gates across stairwells and covers for electrical outlets.

Be prepared for some personal requirements as well. You may be asked for references and proof that you've had vaccinations and haven't had certain contagious diseases. In addition, you must not ever have been convicted for child abuse.

The laws vary tremendously from state to state.

California is especially strict, while other states, like Iowa, have few if any requirements. You may also be affected by regulations set by your local fire, health and zoning departments.

How Many Kids?

Your license may dictate the number of children you may take into your home. Your business sense may do the same thing.

Although most licenses permit up to six children in a day-care home, a recent study found that half the homes in the country actually take in fewer than that. Some parents are willing to pay more for a low child/adult ratio to insure that their children get plenty of attention. Other parents may prefer a larger group because they believe social development is important.

You should decide what will work best for you based on your own feelings and the going rate in your town for smaller and larger group settings. In most day-care homes, the child/adult ratio is small enough to allow you to really get to know each child's developmental level and personality — and that's one of the big rewards of operating this kind of business.

Your New Decor

Once you know what's required, you can go to work equipping your home for your business.

You'll want one area set aside just for children: "not a living room filled with trinkets," Thorensen comments. What's called for is an open area where children can freely move about and play.

Ideally there will be a group space within that area with small tables and chairs or just a carpeted circle where everyone can gather together. An area where children can engage in individual activities, such as playing with puzzles or blocks, is also desirable. Open shelving is great for such an area. It allows the kids to make their own decisions in selecting the toys they want — and it's easy for them to put them back when they're finished. It's far superior to a large box where toys get tossed (and are often broken or lost in the process).

You'll need a soft rug for crawlers — and even older kids who tend to spend an inordinate amount of time on the floor. You'll also want a smooth floor for activities like building block towers.

In buying toys for your kids, keep these guidelines in mind:

- Is it strong, safe and durable? Avoid toys with removable parts, sharp edges, or brittle plastic.

- Is it easy to keep clean? Some day-care providers clean toys by putting them through their automatic dishwashers.

- Does it appeal to the senses?

- Can it be held or grasped easily?

- What age group will it appeal to?

• Will it encourage learning or imaginary play?

• Would a homemade substitute be better?

Toys suggested for infants include rattles, crib mobiles, picture books, soft rubber dolls, hard rubber toys for holding and chewing, objects of varying textures that can be touched and felt, stuffed animals, disks or keys on a short string or ring, spoons, boxes of all sizes and shapes, pots and pans, paper towel rolls, soft blocks, nesting toys and stacking toys.

For older children, in addition to the above, consider push and pull toys, a pounding board, musical instruments, kiddie car, rocking horse, toy telephones (don't forget: you'll need two!), bean bags, wooden clothes pins, costumes for dress up, simple puzzles, Play Dough and large rubber animals.

Outside toys include a small wading pool (or large pan), trikes, wagon, sandbox, small slide, swing and a jungle gym or other climbing equipment. You'll want an area big enough to allow the kids to exercise their muscles and enjoy moving around. One of your biggest expenses could be the fence around your yard.

Tina Pyzik and her husband built all their outdoor equipment and the children's cubbies, but bought everything else at garage sales and school stores. "It's a big investment — toys, tables, books, chairs, cots, indoor and outdoor equipment," she says.

Safety

It can't be overemphasized. It's what intelligent

parents will look for first, along with how loving you're going to be with their little angel.

Here are some guidelines:

- Guard rails are essential on all stairs.

- Only lead-free paint should be used anywhere where children play.

- Electrical wall sockets must be covered.

- Portable heaters or fans should not be at floor level.

- Hot pipes must be safely covered.

- You'll need a protective barrier around wood-burning stoves or other heat sources.

- Medicine cabinets and cupboards containing chemicals must be locked.

- Be sure to rid your house and yard of poisonous plants and other hazards

- On field trips by car, see that big kids use seat belts and use restraining seats for little ones.

Illness

As Karen Thorensen says, "This is the big issue in

day care right now.'' It's undeniable: Children in day care get sick more often than children who not in daycare facilties. And adult providers get sick more than the general population.

Without question you should establish strict policies regarding illness, and you may even be required to do so by state law. A policy might stipulate, for example, that a parent must pick up a child within two hours after being notified that they've become ill and that a child with a contagious illness is not allowed to return until 24 hours after a treatment program, such as antibiotics, has begun.

In spite of such policies, you will occasionally have to deal with a sick child, and there will be days when you feel like staying in bed and hiding your own swollen nose under the covers.

Try to provide a cot in a quiet area near a bathroom for children who become ill and must wait for their parents. And don't wait until it's blatantly obvious that a child has a serious illness before calling a parent. If a normally happy child is not doing well — is fussy and crying and nothing seems to work to calm her down — you're completely justified in calling the parent and suggesting the child may be coming down with something. Remember that it's the early stages when an illness is most contagious and that a child's constant crying can be disruptive to the other children.

You should also have a back-up person in mind who can take care of your group when you become ill. Some of the best day-care providers hire such a back up two or three days a month even if they aren't ill. By taking "mental health days" off occasionally, these providers feel they improve the quality of their care and avoid burnout.

Discipline

You'll probably want to set rules for your kids and communicate them clearly. They might include:

- no hurting another child,
- all toys and equipment must be shared,
- no swinging or throwing toys,
- no running in the house.

When confronted with "inappropriate behavior," you'll want to let the older child know how you feel about what he did and give him a chance to explain how he feels and what caused him to act that way. He has to understand the consequences of behavior that breaks the rules. For infants and toddlers, a gentle but firm "that hurts Jessica" and removing the child from the area may be most appropriate. For the most serious offenses, you might want to isolate the child from the group for a short while. If these tactics don't work, the next step is a discussion with the parents.

Emergencies

Your registration forms will be a major help in preparing you for medical emergencies. For every child in your care it is essential that you have the following on file:

- permission slip for emergency medical treatment,
- a history of the child's illnesses, allergies and in-noculations,
- name and phone number of the child's pediatrician,
- phone numbers for people to call if the child becomes ill and must be picked up. Ordinarily this will be the phone numbers for both parents and, in case neither parent can be reached, a back-up person.

THE BUSINESS SIDE OF DAY CARE

There's more to child care than just caring for the kids, of course. As with any business, there are certain procedures you'll need to follow.

From the beginning, you'll need to keep track of every business-related expense: every trip to the convenience store for a gallon of milk, every box of thumb-tacks, your mileage, your utilities, and every receipt from your weekly grocery shopping trip.

You'll need to learn at least the basics about tax deductions, bookkeeping procedures, and quarterly tax returns. A class in running a small business, such as those offered by the Small Business Administration, can be extremely worthwhile.

Professionalism is the key when it comes to dealing with parents. Always schedule an initial interview to answer questions and have your registration form filled out. Tina explains that there are other reasons for the interview as well: "I want to be sure that the child is old enough and ready to be independent and fit in with the existing group,'' she says. She trusts her instincts. Out of the hundreds of kids she's worked with, only one did not fit in and caused disruptions in the group. After a discussion, the child's mother agreed to withdraw her son from care.

The registration form is a convenient way for you to keep all the information you need in one place. It will prevent you from overlooking important questions you need to ask and makes it clear to parents that you know what you're doing. Once you and the parent have agreed that the child will enter your care program you should have the parent sign your form. It specifically sets forth your policies and is a simple contract.

You may question the need for a contract. It's needed because it's often hard for us to set limits on how much we give people we care about, and you're going to grow to care about your children a great deal. If a parent asks you to keep her child late one night, it may be hard for you to say no, even if it means changing plans you had with your family. And if it happens a second time, you may feel that since you've said yes once, you have to say yes again.

With a contract, your limits are set down for you in black and white.

''You have to be prepared for the less-than-perfect parent,'' warns Thorensen. There are parents who are always late picking up their kids, parents who are always two weeks behind in paying you, and parents who call at the last minute and ask if their child can stay at your house until ten that night.

"Most providers get into this business because they care about children, so when a parent asks, they break the rules on behalf of the child. They feel sorry for him. Eventually, though, you'll become resentful of both the child and parent."

Writing a contract forces you to decide in advance how far you're willing to go in bending the rules.

What to Charge

How much you can charge will depend on your adult/child ratio, the age of the children you keep, your reputation, and the going rate for child care in your area. The average fee for children under 2 is about $50 to $105 per week. For older children $40 to $85 is more common. In large cities the rates may be 10 to 15 percent higher, and in rural areas they may be 10 to 25 percent lower. With a smaller group, a carefully designed play area and playground, formal training or other benefits, you can charge more.

In setting your fee, do some market research to find out what others are charging in your area for comparable services. Then figure your expenses. Make a list of fixed expenses, such as your initial investment for toys, books and cots or mats. Then figure out your variable expenses, which are the costs that increase in direct response to the number of kids you serve. These expenses will include food, salaries for extra helpers, and supplies like paper towels and disposable diapers. Once you've got a good idea what your costs will be and what the market will bear, you'll be able to make an intelligent decision on fees. Whatever you charge will, of course, have to be enough to pay you a reasonable salary.

Marketing

Many day-care providers find that getting their name out is one of the hardest parts of opening their business. In day care, as in any other business, marketing is important. Take a clue from the big day-care chains like Kinder Care and Children's World. Before these companies open a new center they study the market, and you should too. They review census data for the area, looking for middle-income households, above-average education levels and a high proportion of working mothers with children under five. "We'll drive through neighborhoods and look for swing sets, empty two-car garages, Big Wheels," says Doug Carneal, a regional director of Children's World. They also investigate rush-hour traffic flow to help pinpoint desirable locations for centers.

This is not to suggest that you spend a lot of money on an elaborate market study, but you do need to locate parents in need of your services. Try a classified ad in your local newspaper and run it for an extended period. Post notices, as Tina Pyzik did, on grocery store bulletin boards and place fliers on car windshields in shopping centers. Notify the personnel offices of local businesses and colleges of your services. Local health clubs can be good spots for your flier, as are medical centers, the library, and of course, children's stores.

Your flier doesn't have to be a work of art, but it should look professional and clearly explain the benefits of your service. Point out your background, goals and philosophy, being sure to note any special emphasis you place on wholesome nutrition, a stimulating and educational environment, or other aspects of the care you provide.

ACTIVITIES

Scheduling

One of the keys to smooth-running day care is organization. You and your children will both benefit from a daily routine. It will give structure to your days and give you the time to prepare for each activity as it comes along. You'll be able to provide a variety of activities and learning experiences and yet allow time for spontaneity and special events.

Schedules will vary according to the ages of the kids you care for, but a typical schedule might look something like this:

7 to 9 a.m.: Children arrive. Each child is individually welcomed. They hang up their coats. The early birds are fed breakfast and help clean up afterwards. After breakfast is free play time.
9 a.m.: Group activity — a time for children to share and settle into the day. You might want to

mark the calendar with the date and talk about the week's theme or do finger plays or music.

9:30 a.m.: Individual, self-directed play in the playhouse area or with puzzles, blocks, beads, costumes. Or time for art work.

10 a.m.: Mid-morning snack

10:30 a.m.: Outdoor play

11 a.m.: Helpers arrive to prepare lunch

11:40 a.m.: Bathroom and clean up

Noon: Lunch

1 p.m.: Story time or quiet music and singing

1:30 to 3:30 p.m.: Nap time

3:30 p.m.: Snack

4 p.m. to departure: free play as parents arrive

This schedule is flexible and yet it allows you to prepare each day's activities in advance. It may take twice as long as you expected to bake muffins as a group. Or Timmy may have an accident for the first time in a month. You can take it all in stride and enjoy the extra time Sophia needs to make sure the batter is mixed just right. Maybe the kids will have a little less time to play outside or lunch will be delayed a bit, but nobody is likely to mind.

You'll also want to be flexible enough to permit field trips, special visitors and parties. You may want to invite a Jewish parent to share some matzah and explain Passover, or maybe you have a friend who would enjoy showing her pet ferret to the kids. In the fall, you might visit a nearby farm and pick pumpkins out of the field. Weekly trips to the library's story hour or a nearby swim school can be arranged. Picnics, sledding trips, daily walks to a nearby playground or park all add variety to your routine and let the children know there's a big world out there and you care enough to share it with them.

Planning is the key to successful field trips. Parents should be forewarned to pack a change of clothing and you should load up with a first aid kit, extra towels and washrags, plastic bags, toys, food, containers for new-found treasures and perhaps a blanket to sit on. The following questions can help you plan your field trips:

- Who will participate? What ages is it best suited for, and how can it be adapted for those older or younger?

- When is the best time for the activity?

- Where is it and how will you get there? What transportation arrangements need to be made?

- What supplies, materials and equipment will be needed?

- What kind of help will you need? Would another adult make the trip safer or more fun?

Naps

Little children may fight it, but they do need to nap. Ideally you'll have a quiet place to lay them down that's within ear shot. Older children may not be required to nap, but they, too, should have quiet times scheduled for resting and reading. If nothing else they may be allowed to go outside and play while the babies are in dreamland.

Going Potty

You may decide to take only children who are potty trained, or you may find that there is more demand in your area for centers caring for toddlers still in diapers.

If you are expected to be the potty-trainer, don't push it. With your understanding and encouragement, each child will learn and graduate from diapers at his or her own pace. He may even learn to do so more quickly in a day-care setting where all around there are role models who have mastered the art of announcing "I have to go potty" — and then actually do it themselves.

Karen Murphy recommends letting the trainee run bare-bottomed. "Invite" him to use the potty every hour or so for about a week. Use a diaper at nap time only. "When the child makes trips to the bathroom on his own, usually during the second week, he is trained."

Music

Music can be educational, entertaining, calming or fun. A special song can be your signal to the group that it's time to pick up toys or it's time for lunch. Your library can probably lend you a wide variety of records and tape cassettes.

Art

Cottonball snowmen in winter, construction paper spiders in spring, woven paper placemats at any time, a dearly scribbled card for Mother's Day. Art activities show children that they are imaginative and creative individuals with the power to bring their conceptions to life.

If you're tempted to spend a lot of money for art and craft supplies you should realize that much will be wasted or lost. You can often use your imagination to find substitutes for expensive supplies. Try to improvise, and ask your friends and your kids' parents to save their egg cartons, computer print outs, fabric scraps, ribbon, trimmings, yarn and string.

Costumes

No one is suggesting that you visit a costume shop with checkbook in hand, but kids do love to dress up. The solution, again, is to improvise. Get the word out to your kids' parents that you need old hats, belts, scarves, costume jewelry and the like. In time you will accumulate a storage bin that will be an imaginative child's delight on a rainy day.

Activity Centers

A corner for mutually loved and cared-for pets can provide hours of pleasure. Hamsters, goldfish, possibly a pet rabbit or two are a worthwhile addition to your center.

A water table is good for endless hours of pouring, measuring and, hopefully, only a moderate amount of splashing.

A reading corner is a special gift for your children. It can simply be a well lit mound of pillows or a comfortable chair where they can escape for some solitary — or shared — Dr. Seuss.

A science center might be as simple as a magnet, a magnifying glass, and various teasures you've collected on your outings: a robin's egg, brightly colored seed pods, smoothly polished stones from a stream bed.

Preschool

Day-care homes are becoming increasingly involved in pre-reading, pre-math, and pre-science skill development. In fact, some day-care providers offer specialized preschools, meeting three mornings a week for two to four hours. Preschools offer directed activities within a more structured time frame. They emphasize fine muscle development, eye-hand coordination, manipulative skills and alphabet and number recognition.

At Greentree, for example, Tina Pyzik offers "a preschool with extended day care. Day care implies all-day, but less of a learning situation," she explains. Her program emphasizes numbers, the alphabet, the sound of letters and lessons in science.

Tina picks a theme for each week and posts it on her bulletin board: fall, frost, harvest, Valentine's Day, community helpers. Every day during the morning group time the week's topic is discussed, and art projects during the week relate to this theme. In this way Tina gives her kids a taste of social studies and science.

Of course this type of structure may not appeal to you, and the schedule above may be more than you care to deal with. If so, fine. There are many, many day-care homes across the country that schedule no group activities but do provide a loving environment where kids can simply play (with breaks for meals, snacks and naps).

Nutrition

The U.S. Department of Agriculture will assist you in planning nutritious meals for your children. Not only that, USDA provides financial reimbursement and nutritional training to licensed family day-care providers, averaging $225 per month for up to 23 meals or snacks a day. To qualify for the reimbursement you will, of course, have to keep records of what you serve. For details contact your county extension service.

The following can make your meals and snacks both more enjoyable and more healthful:

- Serve portions that are too small rather than too large (you can always serve seconds). This approach will help you avoid waste.

- Try to avoid foods with preservatives, artificial coloring, caffeine, or excessive sugar.

- Allow families to send food with their children

only if they have special diets dictated by allergies or religious beliefs.

• Notice how the children seat themselves and, if necessary, assign seats so that they eat with a minimum of disruptions and upsets.

• Make sure you don't serve anything too hot.

• Don't fill cups too full.

• Make your meals attractive as well as well balanced.

• Don't rush the children through their meals.

MOVING INTO ACTION

So you're ready to welcome your first child. You've invested in toys, enrolled in the food program, fenced your yard, advertised and you're keeping good records of all your expenses. You've made quite a commitment.

Through all the bruised knees and bruised feelings, the burnt soups and runny noses and 500 readings of *The Cat in the Hat*, remember that you're running a business involving lives. You're in business to provide care in a safe environment to growing, extremely vulnerable children. "Nothing can get in the way of that," as Tina Pyzik says.

"Hang in there," she advises. "If you know this is what you want, stick with it. It's hard."

But it's worth it.

Chapter 4
Toys, Toys, Toys

The incredible popularity of the Cabbage Patch dolls created one of the most remarkable business success stories in recent memory. You probably know about the dolls — for weeks there were stories in the national news media on the incredible lengths to which people would go to buy one. What you probably don't know is the story of the humble beginnings of this now legendary success.

Xavier Roberts considered himself more of a "life sculptor" than a businessman when he took the original version of his dolls to flea markets and art shows. People seemed to like them, and, with a few college friends, Roberts founded Original Appalachian Artworks, Inc. and began marketing the dolls through trade shows. It was largely a learn-as-you-go type of operation. Quoted by *The New York Times* Roberts said, "Buyers would come up to us at the Atlanta Merchandise Mart and say,

'Will you take net 10 or net 30?' We'd say, 'We'll have to get back to you on that.' Then we'd go find out what it meant.''

Today Roberts' BabyLand General Hospital in Cleveland, Georgia continues to produce a high-priced version of the dolls ranging from $125 to $1,000. About 350,000 of these Cabbage Patch Kids have been created over the years, with sales going to $5 million. The vinyl-faced version sold by Coleco Industries is mass produced and sold for about $20 each — and some three million were sold in one twelve-month period.

Roberts wasn't really surprised by his success. "We were a bunch of kids. We didn't know we couldn't do it. We went without lunches and paychecks for a long time. But we imagined how big it would be one day.''

Clearly the Cabbage Patch doll experience was exceptional, but it demonstrates just how much potential exists in the toy market — even for those with little experience.

More than $4 billion is spent annually on toys, but you probably know from experience that too many toys — including many plastic cars, plastic dolls, and plastic "entertainment centers" — break within days after you purchase them. The real opportunities today are in providing an attractive alternative to these shoddy, plastic, mass-marketed toys. Even these toys serve a market, of course; otherwise they wouldn't be in the stores. But market niches also exist for high-quality, carefully crafted toys — toys that are new and imaginative and will withstand years of loving abuse.

MORE THAN PLAYTHINGS

Toys carry children into the richest, most exciting world they will ever enter: the world of their imaginations. A wagon becomes a choo-choo train or a space station. A tent becomes a haven from wild bears — and a sanctuary from a ranting mother. A doll becomes a desperately desired baby brother.

Yet toys do more than inspire a child's fantasies. They help develop concepts like coming and going, appearance and disappearance, winning and losing — and playing fair and according to rules.

"Children are interested in motion, in putting together and taking apart, changing things, inventing, trying out roles, practicing what they already know and collecting things. Playthings that address lasting interests like these speak to the core of child life," says the Bank Street College of Education, an institution in New York City which explores educational theories in a humanistic setting.

With toys, kids hook into their environment. Toys are the means to adventure and diversion — but also to socialization, independence and self-confidence. And they need not be elaborate to serve these powerful purposes.

QUALITY FROM THE PAST

Some of the very best toys are those that have endured from generation to generation, but sometimes it's difficult to find that kind of long-lasting quality today.

Solid wood coaster wagons are one such toy. Al and Lois Hough live in Janesville, Wisconsin, where the Janesville Coaster Wagon was manufactured from 1900 to 1934. The Houghs couldn't find anything comparable to the old Janesville Coaster for their own children, and when Al was nearing retirement and looking for something to do, he created a replica of that toy based on research they had done at the county historical society and the help of a somewhat worn original. "I grew up with a wagon, as did everyone around here," reminisced Al.

It took eight months to finalize the reproduction, tool up, get organized and make some wagons, but at last the Wisconsin Wagon Company was in business. Al continued to work as an executive vice president for a company that manufactured partitions, but gradually the Houghs moved into wagon-making full time.

Their research included their own market survey. "You don't need to invest in expensive commercial research," Al advises. He and Lois visited local toy stores to see what was on the market. They evaluated the market on the basis of their own ability to produce an equal product for less or a better product for slightly more.

"We had no competition, so we opted for the higher priced, better product," he explains. Initially the Hough's wagon sold for $150. (It's now priced at $175.) At the time, the highest priced competitive wagon was $65 at better stores.

Hough believes his price is justified because he has a unique, well crafted product. As the Houghs state in their one-page, full-color brochure, "Durability and utilitarian design were the hallmarks of children's toys enjoyed by past generations. Constructed of solid, natural and strong materials, they could be counted on to last a lifetime and even generations." The new Janesville Coaster Wagon clearly fits that description. Made of solid oak with rubber tires on ball bearing wheels and stainless steel ironwork and fasteners, the wagons have a hard urethane finish, and each takes about six hours to make.

Overcoming Obstacles

Like most people starting a business from scratch, the Houghs were faced with overcoming a series of obstacles. After Al was satisfied with his wagon design, for example, he had to acquire production machinery and equipment. Initially he bought his wood planed and cut to the overall correct size. While that increased the cost of materials, "at least it allowed us to get started," he says. As time went on, he acquired more and more equipment which enabled him to buy his materials in rougher and rougher form. Now, almost all of the operation is in-house.

The next obstacle for the Houghs was marketing, and the first decision was whether to go through dealers or to sell directly to consumers. After looking at their costs and the percentage of their retail price that would go to the dealers if they took that route, the Houghs decided it made more sense to try to sell direct. Al sought the advice of an advertising agency, and based on his own experience in marketing and the advice of the agency, he decided to give advertising in magazines a try. The agency prepared their first ad. The Houghs' small ad budget has forced them to rely on minimum-sized ads. They've learned through experience that such small ads are effective for their purposes, however, and they advertise both more frequently and in more magazines as time goes by.

Wisconsin Wagon Works ads are currently found in some ten magazines, including the *Smithsonian Magazine, Country Journal, Family Journal,* and *The New Yorker.* "The magazine you choose has to be one from which people expect to buy direct, in contrast to ones with ads that say 'Find us at your local department store.'" For the Houghs, *The New Yorker* has proven to be "far and away the most effective." He has learned this because "fortunately most people spontaneously tell you where they saw the ad."

After marketing, the next hurdle was expansion. The wagon business was financed through the Hough family, and Al is confident that that's the way to go. "The key thing is to finance it yourself, or with your family, or through people who are going to be tolerant until you become profitable." In his first two years he drew no money from the business, "period."

The company started small, and the Houghs want to see it stay more or less that way. "Our objective is not to grow into another GM," says Al with a laugh. "We don't want to out-run our resources. We want to grow at a controlled pace to handle our growth with our own capital."

As time has rolled on Al and Lois have rounded out their line of merchandise with other oak products: a pump car, a doll cradle, two scale-model wheelbarrows, a scooter, a walnut or cherry baby cradle, and an oversized Fire Island Coaster wagon and a patio cart, both made to order. Their best-seller is the Toddler, a three-wheeled kiddie car. They sold about 300 of those last year, and about 150 coaster wagons.

Al has this advice to offer beginners in the toy business: "Talk to all the people who have the experience you don't — particularly in production and advertising."

COMPANY PROFILES

It's interesting to see the range of toy businesses that are successful. There's inspiration to be gained from success stories, too, and what worked for somebody else might very well work for you.

Puppy Dog Eyes

Designer Francesca Hoelein was woofing about rejection in 1981. But by early 1983 Franland, her company, had realized more than $6 million in sales from the cuddly, floppy dogs with woeful eyes known as "le Mutt." Le Mutt now has a female friend, Fifi La Femme, and Hoerlein has a partner, William Locton, who borrowed $25,000 from his father to produce and ship the first 700 dozen toy dogs. The 20-inch dogs are manufactured in Taiwan and are sold nationally in major department stores, gift shops and toy shops for about $17, with a smaller version going for $6.95. Franland has now signed licensing agreements with an infant clothing manufacturer and a sleeping bag manufacturer.

Toys With a Purpose

Lane Nemeth launched Discovery Toys six years ago when she retired to have a baby after years as an educator and administrator. She was dismayed at the quality of toys available for her child and put together a broad line of educational toys which includes everything from teething rings and stacking toys to a sand-water mill, safety scissors, a cookbook, a book for grandparents, and lots of art and nature projects. Last year her company, which began in her northern California garage, marked $25 million in sales.

Not an Ordinary Doll

Majorie Spangler has created a company with impressive sales figures from her family's garage in Concord, California. Her company, Marjorie Spangler Dolls, Inc. makes dolls similar to those she made for her children when they were small. Selling for $36 to $140, her porcelain or vinyl dolls are hand-painted and costumed. Unlike ordinary dolls, Marjorie's are beautiful collector-quality dolls including debutante dolls, bride dolls, toddlers and babies in christening dresses, with bonnets and laces, full skirts and curls. The company is "dedicated to the rebirth of fine doll artistry," according to the company slogan. Originally Spangler learned to make doll-baby molds in her kitchen, "but the materials I was using plugged up the plumbing," she recalled — the hazards of self-employment. She moved to the garage as orders from friends and collectors in doll clubs came in. Now Spangler dolls are sold at F.A.O. Schwarz, Bloomingdale's, Neiman Marcus, Broadway Stores, May Company and others.

Bullish on Bears

Barbara Isenberg founded the North America Bear Company in Greenwich, Connecticut in 1978. From a studio in her house she designs stuffed bears and gives them names like Shakesbear and Bearishnikov. Sales have reached the $5.5 million range, and the business has grown to the point where a factory is now required for production.

MORE OBSTACLES TO OVERCOME

Not all businesses in the toy field are unequivical success stories, of course, and there are valuable lessons to learn from companies that readily admit the problems they face.

Toys Made with Love

Dale Prohaska, Jr. makes and markets patterns for people who want to make toy trucks, trains, cars, puzzles and rocking horses. Thanks to his company, parents all over the country can fill their kids' needs for toys while they fill their own needs for being creative and productive.

Love-Built Toys and Crafts began as a part-time business twelve years ago when Prohaska, then a school teacher, made his first patterns. He had seen some wooden toys at a gas station during a trip to Oregon and felt sure he could make better ones. He got the idea that there might be a market for toy patterns from a classified ad he had seen for furniture patterns.

Working from his home, Prohaska developed "toddler-proof" wooden toys which could be made using hand tools without the use of nails or screws. Business grew, and in a few years he quit his teaching job to devote himself fully to his business.

From the very beginning the business has been a learning experience for Prohaska. His first magazine classified ad offered ten patterns for $1 — and didn't include the name to whom his customers should make out their checks! "I had to figure out a way to cash those checks, along with how to reprint patterns, how to handle the hours it took to draw a pattern and basic marketing," he says.

Prohaska's patterns are printed on paper and include instructions, much like sewing patterns. He now markets books on woodworking along with parts for his patterns that aren't available through lumberyards — like wheels, smoke stacks and pegs. His toys have sold to individuals, schools, craft shops, scouting organizations and wholesalers throughout the U.S., Mexico, Canada and Europe, and now he is starting a new company devoted to furniture patterns and parts, along with tools and books.

This may sound like Love Built has no problems, but that's not entirely the case. "The market is still the same size as it was when I began," says Prohaska, who was the first — and only — manufacturer of toy patterns during his first five years in business. But competition has squeezed into his market. "You come up with an idea, and people start to copy you. Now the pie is cut into more slices, so there's less for you."

If he had it to do over again, Prohaska says he'd be a lot more aggressive in marketing his products than he was at first. He spent $500 on advertising his first year in business; his new company will spend $10,000 in its first year.

Classified ads were a cheap way for Prohaska to find his market. It's a way of testing new product ideas without spending a lot of money surveying the market. "If you can describe your product or a brochure about your product in a few words, get it into a classified ad to check the market before you invest big bucks in larger display ads," he suggests.

His company has stayed with small display ads which advertise his catalog. He does not recommend sending potential customers a free catalog "unless you have an extremely high-profit, general-interest item which nearly everyone will want to buy. If you offer a free catalog, you will have many curiosity seekers writing for it," he explains.

The mail-order industry is such that if out of one hundred catalogs mailed out, three people order from it, "that's high," Prohaska says. The average return is half that: one and a half percent. Prohaska urges new business owners to "watch out for inventory. You don't want a lot. You want to be able to restock from suppliers or manufacturers quickly, rather than have 300,000 widgets sitting around waiting for orders." The rule of thumb in mail-order businesses is to charge five times what you paid for a given product to cover expenses. "You can get around that if you have a good relationship with a supplier so that you can fill an order within two or three days without tying up a lot of money in inventory — and expensive bank loans."

Like others who are self-employed, Prohaska says the more help you get when you're starting out, the better. He has taken courses in advertising, management and merchandising.

Prohaska is now developing a wholesale market, and says that "I refuse to print new patterns. I'm looking for new markets for the old ones." Although he broke one-half million dollars in sales last year, his profit, he says, is the same as it was several years ago — small. The business underwent a severe belt-tightening three or four years ago, and another one may be on the way. "I'm trying to stay in business," he says.

"Staying in business" requires the help of the entire Prohaska family. Carolyn Prohaska has worked on advertising and promotion. Dale has been accountant, typist, errand boy, drafting designer, photographer, layout artist and order processor. The Prohaska children are models for patterns and the catalog, and they test all products. "If you don't want to do everything,

don't go into business for yourself," Prohaska advises.
Nevertheless, he doesn't think he would want to
ever again work for anyone else. "The whole experience
of building up this business has been extremely gratifying, from that first toy I built for my son. And it all
started with a $1 pattern."

From Submarines to Rocking Horses

Eight years ago 42-year-old Larry Kuivanen decided to quit his work in submarine design and go to work
on rocking horses and wooden toys instead. "If I could
stop one child from being killed in a war, I knew it
would be worth it," he says. But even with those ideals,
making and marketing toys has not been a bed of roses.

When Kuivanen decided to leave the weapons
design field, "I knew I had to do something." The question was what. He had woodworking equipment; it had
been a hobby for him. He made a rocking horse, and
pretty soon he and his wife Robin were making more of
them in the basement of their Connecticut home.

The business grew, and a toy chest, toy trains and
wagons were added to the product line. The Kuivanens
decided to market their products wholesale. "To
manufacture for retail is difficult because you have a
limited amount of traffic," Larry points out. You need
a well rounded line of products, or a very unique product like the Janesville Coaster Wagon. With only seven
toys in their line at the time, the Kuivanens opted for the
wholesale market and took their wares to trade shows.

In 1981 they changed horses, so to speak, and

eliminated toys from their line. Now their only product is a child's wooden chair with a canvas seat marketed through catalogs like Horchow, Joan Cook and Geary's and through sales reps at all the national juvenile trade shows.

"In 1981 the profits were just not there for toys," Kuivanen said. "We had a lot of employees making 32 items. The chair was selling, so we decided to go with it exclusively."

A number of factors, including rising costs of liability insurance for toy manufacturers, tightening government regulations and rising overseas competition combined to drive Kuivanen out of the toy business. Even with the chair, competition is a major problem. Copies manufactured in Taiwan for about half of Kuivanens' cost are now being marketed in the U.S. His chairs cost him $7.50 to make and retail for $17; he figures the imported models cost about $4.

Yet sales are up for "Just Wood." For the first seven months of 1984, sales almost matched the total sales figures for all of 1983. With different colors, silk-screen designs and names on the chairs, Kuivanen has diversified his product. Now he believes his success hinges on finding a reliable and reasonable materials supplier, which he says is a must for any self-employed manufacturer. Primarily because of new housing starts, the price of lumber recently jumped 20 percent in a two month period, with predictable effects on Kuivanen's profit margin.

Selling smiles is clearly a struggle for Kuivanen. "The product has got to be right," he says. "You ought to be able to get a good price for a good product. But the profit margin is not what it should be.''

SOME THINGS TO CONSIDER

Hopefully Kuivanen will find the right supplier and his sales will continue to grow. In any case, don't be too discouraged by his experience. Just realize that succeeding in *any* business will require facing up to problems and doing your best to overcome them.

If you think producing creative, high-quality toys is the business you'd like to try, here are a few things you'll need to consider.

Safety

An estimated 70,000 children are sickened, injured or even killed by their playthings each year. Common sense dictates many precautions and the Consumer Product Safety Commission (CPSC) has established the following as guidelines for toy safety:

- No sharp edges or points (including corners). Avoid exposed pins, nails, wires, screws — anything that could conceivably cause cuts, scrapes, or puncture wounds. Wooden toys must be sanded smooth, and preferably given a protective finish, in order to eliminate splinters.

- No exposed mechanical parts or small, removable parts that can easily be swallowed. Parts that can come off, like eyes and buttons on stuffed dolls and animals, must be securely fastened. Squeakers in squeeze toys must be secured inside.

• Within reason, toys should be unbreakable. Avoid flimsy or brittle plastic, glass, or any other material which might shatter, splinter, or otherwise break.

• According to the CPSC, paint used on toys must not contain more than .06 percent lead.

Durability

Remember that the market is already saturated with cheap toys that quickly show the effects of use (or simply break before they've had a chance to age gracefully). Today's consumers have an eye for high quality, well constructed products. They're often willing to pay a premium for toys that they're sure will last through all the misuse they will be subjected to.

Age Appropriateness

"Children are not merely small versions of adults, but changing human beings with special maturing tasks to accomplish as they grow," according to the Bank Street College. Each task is accomplished in its proper place in the long and complex road we call development, and just as a clothing manufacturer has to consider the size of his customers, toy makers must market their products to the appropriate age group.

Here's a list of age-appropriate toys to get you thinking. Remember, the best toys are geared to a child's size and age and require little or no instruction, supervision or maintenance.

Infancy

During the first six months, toys play an important part in stimulating a baby's senses. She needs fun things to look at, touch and chew on and since she spends a lot of time lying on her back, don't forget about toys which hang from the ceiling or side of the crib. Mobiles, music boxes, shiny balls and rattles, soft toys and crib activity centers are popular among the under-one-year-old set. And, of course, infants love stuffed animals.

Later, crawling toys that baby can push on all fours, rolling toys and stacking toys are appropriate.

One Year

With increased mobility and the ability to walk, it's time for a rocking horse, pull toys, small gym sets, indoor sponge toys for throwing, bath toys, toys that open and shut and early musical toys. The Bank Street College suggests, "They need toys that are comfortable for plump hands with small fingers, eyes that are not yet fully developed, curious minds that comprehend only a small portion of a limited 'here and now' world."

Two Years

By two, he's riding small push toys, sculpting with clay and drawing, climbing like a monkey, pushing dolls in a carriage, scooping and digging and pounding. A two-year-old can put together a rudimentary puzzle, can climb and stack big blocks and is ready for the smaller ones in geometrical shapes.

Three Years

At three she wants big trucks or vehicles on which to ride, beanbags to toss, snap-together blocks with which to build. The wonderful world of make-believe is opening up. *The Ultimate Baby Catalog* notes that "Fantasies play a key role in your baby's development, and the most important of all the inhabitants in that world are dolls and stuffed animals."

Three-year-olds want toys that clarify the daily events of their lives as they grow in awareness of themselves.

Four Years

Make-believe becomes slightly more sophisticated now. Pretend kitchens and Western main streets are in order, along with costumes and props. It's time to cut and paste. Miniatures of the real world are very popular at this age, along with real working tools, more sophisticated puzzles and blocks, peg boards, and sewing.

Five Years

Time for art supplies, games and crafts, and collections of all kinds. Kites and swings are enjoyed to the fullest, along with games with rudimentary sets of rules.

Six Years

It's the age of clubhouses or secret hideaways, dolls that wet their diapers and drink from bottles. Sixes can begin more advanced crafts like woodworking, weaving, knitting. They love competition in the form of jacks or marbles. They want a sled, stilts, roller skates and every chance they can get to run, climb, jump — move! They may begin learning tennis or skiing, and certainly they're well up on two-wheeled bikes by now.

Seven to Thirteen

Now comes jigsaw puzzles, complex models, all kinds of sports and games. Games teach children to be responsive, to understand others' points of view and to coordinate their thinking with the thinking of others. And, of course, they're fun, whether it's as simple as "king of the mountain" or as complex as the newer computer games. Pre-teens need toys that challenge their rapidly developing minds and bodies.

Along with age-appropriate marketing, consider two other factors in appealing to parents on behalf of kids: self-confidence and ethnic background. Can your toy somehow help a child feel good about what he can do and his place in the world? Subtle messages about what a boy or girl can or cannot do, messages which perpetuate racist or sexist stereotypes, are increasingly resented by well educated consumers.

GENERATING IDEAS

As in any home business, the toy business you're likely to be most successful at is apt to be the one that most involves what you enjoy. Like to work in wood like Al Hough? Design cute stuffed animals like Frencesca Hoelein? Create new wooden toy designs like Dale Prohaska? Do you draw? Love fabrics? Many self-employed people literally put their hobbies to work for them when they started their businesses.

Walk through any toy store — in fact, walk through many toy stores and toy departments — and check out what's selling and what's not. Talk to parents and teachers to learn what's available and what's lacking. And, above all, talk to kids.

Most home-manufactured toys are wooden: trucks with colorful, removable bottles or people, teethers, puzzles, pull toys, stacking toys, blocks. Also on the market are puppets and dolls, of course, from soft rag dolls to amazingly realistic furry animals and wooden families that fit together like a three-dimensional hug.

Other handcrafted toys speak to special needs. "Bestfriends," of Winter Park, Colorado, introduces children to the realities of handicaps. The soft dolls include a smiling, one-legged skier, a hugable redhead with dark glasses and a seeing eye dog, a tennis player with a leg brace. And, of course, educational toys are booming in popularity, from movable toys for teaching eye-hand coordination in infants to software that teaches computer literacy through fun.

Play is a natural and essential part of life. Somehow toys manufactured because their creator had an inspiration about what could be fun seem more enjoyable than gimmicks that just add clutter to the house. If you have an idea that you believe in and the persistence to bring it to reality, it might bring joy to a child's heart — and a profitable new career to you.

In summary, remember to:

• Target your market. Know whom you're selling to, where your buyers are located and how best to reach them, whether it's through retailing, wholesaling, or mail-order catalog sales.

• Have an original idea. "Otherwise your initial lack of creativity will persist throughout your whole business," advises puppet maker Sue Rigdon.

• Don't go full time at first unless you are well capitalized.

• Keep your overhead as low as possible.

• Talk to as many experts as you can, including

someone with accounting expertise, but don't hire on-going professional help until you need it.

• Expect to do everything from designing to manufacturing to sweeping up. It's all up to you, at least in the beginning.

OTHER POSSIBILITIES

Although the focus of this chapter is on creating and marketing your own high-quality toys, other opportunities exist which may be even more appealing to you.

Perhaps the idea of owning a toy store seems unimaginative and old-hat to you, but some people are busily proving that toy retailing — and toy renting — can be both highly creative and profitable. Here are just a few examples.

Literally a Zoo

When Arthur Watson retired from his position as Baltimore's first zookeeper in 1981, he opened a different kind of zoo. Arthur Watson's Embraceable Zoo is located in a 338-square-foot store in Baltimore's new Harbor Place, and the tiny size of the shop has made creativity essential. An architect was hired to design shelves for imaginatively displaying the animals without wasting space, and restocking is necessary two or three times a day from Watson's $30,000 inventory.

There's something poetic about a retired zookeeper opening such a unique shop, but Watson is getting more from his efforts than just the companionship of his stuffed animals. With annual sales of around $400,000, he's making after-tax profits of about 12 percent.

Cabbage Patch Again

Michael Katz and Jeanette Rush figured the folks wanting Cabbage Patch dolls deserved better treatment than having to be placed on store waiting lists — some of which were ridiculously long. Setting out to remedy the situation, the two partners opened The Doll Patch store in San Francisco, a store that sells only Cabbage Patch Kids.

But The Doll Patch is a doll store with a difference. Katz and Rush arrange for doctors and nurses — who are really theatre students wearing the appropriate costumes — to deliver the dolls into the waiting arms of proud "parents." Doll buyers are required to take an oath of adoption, promising they will give their dolls love with all their hearts. A Polaroid shot of the delivery and adoption ceremony is a free added touch.

Are people really willing to pay for such theatrics? Apparently so — after only six weeks in business Katz and Rush had reportedly broke even on their $40,000 investment.

A Different Kind of Library

Janice and Jon Bergstrom of Norwich, Vermont were amazed at their sons' begging for toys that they actually enjoyed for only a short while. "I just looked at

all the slightly used toys the kids had wanted desperately
— and then suddenly tired of,'' marveled Jon.

Realizing that parents everywhere experienced the
same problem, the Bergstroms came up with the idea of
a Toybrary — a place where kids (and adults) could borrow new playthings much as they borrow books from a
library. Members of Toybrary are issued red-and-white
membership cards which give them access to an estimated $700,000 worth of tricycles, trucks, teeter-totters,
trampolines, telescopes and almost 1,500 other items.

Toybrary fees range from $100 for families to
$1,600 for hotels (schools, camps and hospitals have
also joined). All members sign a form agreeing to
replace or repair broken toys. During the first three
months of business over 400 people signed up for
membership.

Most items can be borrowed for two-week periods,
although certain professional equipment has a one-week
time limit. Most of the inventory is generally out at any
given time, so members browse by looking through a
35mm slide show or computerized list of the toy inventory.

In addition to the income from memberships,
revenue is generated from late fees and software fees.
More important, though, is the number of inquiries the
Bergstroms have received regarding franchising. So far
four franchises have actually been sold. Franchisees pay
about $10,500 for an area with a population of 125,000,
plus a 5 percent royalty fee on gross annual revenues. In

addition, about $100,000 is required for inventory.

Whichever approach appeals to you — whether it's producing high-quality hand-crafted toys or opening a new type of toy shop — with enough determination and imagination you can find a niche in the toy market that will work for you.

Chapter 5
Everybody Loves Camp

"The squeals of delight around the swimming pools of summer camps in the months ahead will no doubt drown out the adding machines in the camp offices — but just barely."
— Jeannye Thornton
U.S. News and World Report

"I can't think of a better profession."
— camp owner/director Don Cheeley

Camping has become a 3.5 billion dollar business for the 10,000 camps in the U.S. which cater to everyone from computer whizzes to cheerleaders, from budding soccer stars to overweight depressives — and even a few normal kids who just want to sing around campfires and learn crafts in a beautiful setting.

It can be a uniquely satisfying business venture. Running a camp is being in the business of "character building, growth promoting," as third generation camp owner/director Don Cheeley puts it. Although inflation is taking more of a bite than it used to, profits are up. Even during the recent recession, only a handful of camps across the country failed, and camp operations can be temptingly profitable. In Massachusetts a private camp for boys grosses $800,000 a year, while a string of six camps owned by a family in the Ozarks grosses $1 million annually.

If you don't have a magnificent natural setting nearby that you can turn into a full-fledged summer camp, don't despair. Day camps are flourishing on rooftops in New York City and in pocket parks across America. A day camp can become a low-overhead, close-to-home enterprise for you. This chapter will consider both residential camps and day camps, beginning with conventional residential camps.

RESIDENTIAL CAMPS

Without the tax exemptions of nonprofit camps, with no subsidies unless social service agencies underwrite expenses for low-income children, and with sky-high insurance rates, camp owners are like virtually all other small business people in bemoaning their rising costs. Lynn Walker estimates that one summer of high quality programming at her Trojan Ranch Camp costs $200,000. Insurance alone costs about $25,000, but that's not the biggest expense. Food for 700 campers and maintenance of pool, horses, equipment, buildings and four large school buses eat up the biggest part of the budget.

Yet Trojan Ranch charges only $250 a week for the residential camp and $80 for its five-day-a-week day camp. That's the low end of the mid range as far as camp fees go — residential camp fees generally range from about $180 to $375 a week. The camp pays land taxes and summer salaries for the Walkers and "gives us our home." All family members except Lynn, who runs the camp year-round, work city jobs in the winter.

The Walkers are in the business simply because "We love it. We love children. This is our second family."

Both Lynn Walker and Don Cheeley operate camps which have been in their families for years. Trojan Ranch has been operating at its present location since 1947, when it was started by Lynn Walker's father-in-law. Cheeley camps have been in business for 64 years; they were begun by Don Cheeley's grandfather.

Launching a Camp: Accreditation

The American Camping Association (ACA) grew out of the Camp Directors' Association which was founded in 1902 to promote healthful and safe camps. In 1948 the ACA capped 13 years of discussion by adopting a set of standards to accredit camps in safety and efficiency.

Today, 230 standards reflecting quality of personnel, facilities, administrative procedures, site and programming fill a 78-page book designed to aid camps, parents and the millions of kids who attend camps in this country every summer. Although some states inspect camps, the ACA is the only organization with a national program that can be applied to a wide variety of camps (including day camps, residential camps, private camps, church camps, travel camps, adventure camps, and camps for people with special needs).

To become accredited, you, as camp director, first join the ACA, pay your dues and a service fee based on your income, and sign a statement of ethics. Next you attend an ACA orientation to review the standards. Finally, a team visits your camp while it is in session. According to Nancy Kolberstein of the ACA, in the course of the six-to-eight hour visit the team will tour the site, inspect facilities, and review "a great amount of paperwork like safety procedures and personnel policy brochures." They check water purity, waste disposal, safe storage of foods and dangerous equipment and substances, health records, cleaning of food service utensils, emergency transportation, toilet facilities, sleeping accommodations and supervision of activities.

"It's quite detailed," says Kolberstein.

The goal, she says, is to ensure a quality camping experience. "We want the child to come away feeling good about himself, having learned new skills, having learned to live and work with other people in the outdoors."

About seven percent of the camps visited each year do not meet the criteria for accreditation, according to ACA officials. While they may not advertise themselves as accredited, they may reschedule another ACA team visit the following summer. In any event, each camp is visited every three years to undergo the accreditation process again.

You can get a fairly accurate picture of what running a camp entails just by considering each of the categories the ACA evaluates in their accreditation procedure.

Programming

The goal of programming is to provide "experiences which will foster human dignity, facilitate the developmental tasks of a camper and enhance social relationships," according to the ACA. A daily routine provides the structure and stability of a camp. Campers awaken to reveille, eat breakfast, make their beds, and have hourly, supervised activities interspersed with meals, rest periods and free time. Special events are generally organized each evening after dinner, and daily special events provide variety.

Trojan Ranch, like most camps its size, offers a broad range of programmed activities. Although the exact programming varies depending on each summer's staffing, typical offerings include activities in Western riding, animal care (horses, goats and pigs), swimming, archery, riflery, arts and crafts, rowing, gymnastics, organic gardening, nature, environmental awareness, hiking and camping, New Games, creative dramatics, movie making, aerobics, soccer, and specialty areas of martial arts.

The ACA requires "breadth" in three or more program areas. Free play, instruction, practice sessions, novelty activities, special events and activities integrated with other program areas are used to give that "breadth." Campers should be involved with program planning and should be encouraged to initiate their own activities. In other words, the camp must provide opportunities for choice, flexibility, and responsibility.

A new trend in camping is the addition of computers, both as an administrative tool and as a program area. Technical climbing, windsurfing and use of some of the new three-wheeled recreational vehicles are also being added to some camp programs.

The ACA wants programs to help campers develop an appreciation of ecology, quality of environment, open space, and natural resource use. Programs must stimulate campers intellectually and socially and help them to develop conversational skills and consideration for others; to help make friends and to feel comfortable with new people. Programs should also encourage campers to extend themselves physically.

Personnel

"The staff really determines the effectiveness of the camp," according to the ACA. "They're the key to a quality camp," Cheeley adds.

To be accredited by the ACA, the camp director (presumably you) must be at least 25 years old, with a bachelor's degree, recent education in camping or environmental studies, and supervisory experience in an organized camp.

Most of the couselors must be at least 18; some must hold bachelor's degrees and all must be at least two years older than the campers with whom they work. Each counselor must be interviewed prior to employment, and the ACA sets guidelines for acceptable counselor/camper ratios.

Lynn Walker says a good counselor is sincere, warm, caring, interested in children, and willing to work "long, hard hours in the outdoors. This is not a 9-to-5 job. You have to be able to live and work together 24 hours a day, seven days a week." Most of her staff is experienced at camp work, although "that's not absolutely necessary because it doesn't tell the whole story." That's why she asks about family history during staff interviews. She also gives interviewees some hypothetical situations to see how they'd react to emergencies or problems that arise with campers, like homesickness and disagreements. "While we're interviewing, we feel them out and anticipate how they'll function together," she explained.

Cheeley, also, looks for high caliber counselors "who are interested in kids and who have skills to teach." In fact, he believes that hiring good people and investing in staff training is one of the best business investments a camp director can make. "You have to operate as a business to keep costs in line. Good, sound decisions and investments, like staff training, are one way to do that."

How do you find counselors you can depend on? The Walkers visit local college campuses to recruit, advertise in the national ACA directory and hire campers who have participated in their counselor-in-training program or have heard about the camp from friends who have worked there.

The ACA requires that each counselor have at least two hours daily away from the job and 24 hours off each week or 48 consecutive hours off every two weeks. Staff must have a place to get together away from campers. A pre-camp training program must include time to get acquainted, become familiar with the program and resources, learn procedures, and understand objectives. In-service programs must be regularly scheduled and include meetings, skills training sessions, and a library.

There are detailed ACA standards for specific program areas like horse riding, water sports, etc. Generally speaking, though, the guidelines specify that leaders have skills appropriate to the activity and have competence in judging the limitations and abilities of campers.

After all, as Lynn points out, "on one level or another, everything we do is high risk, be it horses, riflery, archery." A week-long staff orientation before the kids arrive teaches the "close and constant" supervision practiced at Trojan Ranch. Instructors and counselors accompany every group of campers through every activity, so there is actually double supervision. "We've had no serious injuries," Lynn says.

Site

Camps are meant to be places where stress is reduced, and a safe, peaceful, close-to-nature environment is an important part of the camping experience. The ACA wants a written master site plan for the development and management of camp land, buildings, and utilities. The site must provide natural resources for an enriching, outdoor living experience, and the camp must provide a plan for controlling the quality of the environment at the site. There must also be a written plan that identifies natural and manmade hazards, establishes regulations, and provides for the elimination of those hazards.

Further requirements include fire, risk, motor vehicle, and comprehensive liability insurance coverage, inventories of all facilities and equipment, and annual inspections and procedures for fire protection with an inventory of all fire extinguishers, firefighting equipment, and fire areas.

Food areas must be well lit and ventilated, easy to maintain and free of rodents and "vermin." Sleeping units must be cross-ventilated, must have fire escapes, and must have a specified amount of space per person. Toilets must be clean, well ventilated and adjacent to handwashing facilities, and there must be enough warm water for bathing everyone in camp.

Administrative Procedures

The ACA requires that each camp have a written statement of goals with specific objectives for camper development.

Don Cheeley summarizes his goals as "fun-plus," a

program which places a value on campers developing strong friendships worldwide, overcoming obstacles such as lack of self-confidence or self-esteem, and learning new skills and becoming responsible for their actions. Lynn Walker says the goal of Trojan Ranch is "to provide a wholesome, learning, and growing experience in the outdoors."

Evaluation procedures and parent-camp communication are required by the ACA. Written records on campers should include health histories and records, and you'll also be required to have written personnel policies, job descriptions, a budget and records of menus, purchases, inventories, and equipment.

Personnel with current American Red Cross first aid certification (or its equivalent) must be at the camp at all times, and you'll need to make arrangements with a nearby physician or hospital in case of emergencies. Narcotics and other medications must be locked and dispensed only under specified direction from a licensed physician, and a written outline of procedures for health supervision is required.

Additional ACA requirements relate to provisions for emergency communications, menu plans, food storage, sewage and garbage disposal, and motor vehicle service.

Specialized Residential Camps

There's a specialized camp for practically every child today, whether he or she is overweight, brilliant, shows athletic promise, or is pursuing a particular interest such as classical music or computer programming. A quick scan of the ACA's *Parents' Guide to Accredited Camps* shows camps that focus on tennis, reading, outdoor skills, gymnastics, scuba and water sports, Judaism, wilderness experiences, art, self-awareness and self-improvement, Christianity, riding, performing arts, travel, weight loss, cheerleading, team sports, academics, and numerous other fields. Specially designed camps that cater to children with diabetes, developmental disabilities and learning disabilities also exist, and other camps cater to entire families.

Specialization is clearly a growing trend in camp programming. A look at a few of the more popular types of specialty camps gives some idea of the possibilities.

Sport Camps

Camps focusing on competitive sports require qualified instructors to teach both basic skills and advanced techniques. Some camps hire athletic stars to lend prestige to their programs and gain a marketing advantage. The four locations of the Offense-Defense Football Camps, for example, feature two- or three-day coaching sessions with pros like "Mean" Joe Greene and "Too Tall" Jones. "What kids learn from a pro sinks in more," says camp director Mike Meshken.

Some campers complain about the fierce competition at group sport camps. Camps that specialize in noncompetitive sports seem more low-key, although the program can be just as focused. At one riding camp, reported a mother, "Everything the girls did was horse-related. During crafts sessions they made bridles. They swam almost solely to get the smell of horses off their bodies." Other riding camps purposely limit the time campers spend riding and caring for their horses in an effort to provide a more balanced camp experience.

Academic Camps

"Exploration," which offers high schoolers workshops on topics ranging from radio drama to the decision-making process of the Supreme Court, meets on the campus of Wellesley College in Massachusetts. Other camps are aimed at gifted children or children who want a head start in college. There are also camps intended for kids who need help maintaining their appropriate academic level and camps for children with learning disabilities.

Some academic camps are even further specialized in their offerings. Seacamp in Big Pine Keys, Florida, for example, offers workshops for kids interested in becoming future marine scientists. Campers take labs in marine geology, vertebrates and oceanography, and even dive with professional marine biologists.

Most camps, however, just add a smattering of academics to what is essentially a conventional camp program. It's a way to please everyone: the kids, who mainly want to swim, ride horses, and otherwise have fun — and the parents, who want to justify the expense as a worthwhile contribution to their children's education.

Computers

Computer camps are still a relatively new type of specialty camp, but their impact shouldn't be underestimated. Some 100,000 Americans will attend computer camp this year.

Residential computer camps typically serve kids in the 9-to-17 age bracket. Most programs last a week or two, with at least three hours of computer instruction per day.

At the better camps, a great deal of individual attention is offered. Campers work on individualized projects based on their own abilities and interests, and there is plenty of time for experimenting with the equipment.

Most computer camps strive for a balance between using computers and participating in other, more traditional camp activities. The problem, though, is that "the kids tend to get hooked," according to Dennis Dempsey, co-director of the Sun Valley Computer Camp. "We don't want them to spend nine hours a day in front of the computer, which is what they'd do if we let them. We have to say, 'No more, we're going swimming.' "

Art Camps

From camps requiring taped auditions to camps where the youngsters have barely mastered "Chopsticks," art camps span the spectrum of theater, performing arts, visual art and music. A camp in Connecticut offers a weekly magazine, radio station, jazz band, symphony, chamber and pit orchestras, clown workshop, and lessons in puppetry, ballet, modern dance, and theater.

A Chapel Hill camp produces eight musicals and dramas "for the developing actor." Marrowstone Music Festival permits campers accepted by audition to play for three weeks on the spectacular Olympic Penninsula, supervised by University of Washington music professors. Apple Farm Arts and Music Center not only produces concerts and theatrical productions — its campers also milk cows and work in the garden.

Health Camps

While special camps cater to children with asthma, diabetes, and emotional and physical development problems, the best-known health camps are dedicated to weight loss. Such camps usually serve well balanced, low-calorie meals and offer classes on nutrition, eating behavior, and exercise. The more effective camps deal with positive visualization, body image, eating habits, and a wide variety of exercise options as well. About 25 weight camps are accredited by the ACA, and all are located in lovely rustic settings with programs including dramatics, journalism, music, roller skating, horseback riding, riflery, photography, and fine arts. Most offer poise and body-building classes and some have follow-up programs or monthly newsletters to help campers maintain weight loss when they get home.

Losing weight is hardly ever easy, but with the controlled environment of a specialized camp many kids manage to lose impressive amounts. The positive effects can extend beyond the immediate health benefits, too. As one obesity expert says, ''Once a child sees the difference in his appearance and the favorable reactions of friends and family as a result of controlled eating habits, it gives them a feeling of self-confidence.''

Experts warn against hiring counselors who are overweight themselves. Most of the counselors at weight camps are professionals affiliated with a group like Weight Watchers International.

Campers must be strongly encouraged to participate in the exercise program at weight camps. ''The one thing we don't allow is spectator-itis,'' says Thelma Hurtwitz, who has operated weight camps for more than 10 years on five campuses throughout the Northeast. At the Hurtwitzes' Camp Camelots, a diet nutritionist and consultant to the New York State Department of Health created the menu plan. Daily classes in nutrition and aerobics are mandatory, as well as a weekly private meeting with the camp nutritionist. Girls study good grooming, and boys take calisthenics, body building and weightlifting, along with a full range of indoor and outdoor sports, arts and crafts.

Attracting Campers (Marketing)

Suppose you've got your American Red Cross-certified water instructors and your computer whiz who fortunately loves kids and knows how to get through to them. How do you go about lining up campers?

Accreditation helps, especially for a new camp. If other camps in your area are full they're apt to look in the ACA directory and refer parents to other ACA camps in the vicinity. Parents themselves may also look through the directory and conclude that you're in exactly the location where they want to drive this summer — and they'll drop Johnny off while they're in the neighborhood.

Don Cheeley and his wife travel 13,000 miles through fourteen states every winter showing slides to former campers who, hopefully, will bring along their friends who might want to give Cheeley Camps a whirl.

Both Cheeley and Lynn Walker agree that return enrollment and word of mouth are their best advertisements. Alumni (often parents or, in Cheeley's case, even grandparents) will send their kids to the camp they fondly remember attending. Cheeley sends birthday and Christmas cards to his alumni, along with a newsletter he publishes five times a year.

Camp fairs, which are held in cities around the country, can also be good sources of new campers. Cheeley sends parents to represent him at fairs in their area, and he pays them a commission for each child they sign up, applicable to their own child's tuition.

DAY CAMPS

If you're stuck in the city wondering how to augment your income while shaking your head over the kids hanging around the corner fire hydrant, maybe you should consider starting a day camp. Those running residential camps also find that day-camp programs can nicely complement their existing programs. In the 1950s, for example, the Walkers realized that Trojan Ranch could accommodate ninety additional kids by adding a day-camp program.

Richard Brown made the decision to start a day camp while he was still in high school. "The first summer we worked really hard, and we made $400 apiece for the whole summer," he recalls. Four years later he and his two sisters had multiplied their earnings by ten, and they were paying other siblings and aids they employed as well. "We had waiting lists," he says.

Day camps make it possible for kids to enjoy a camp experience even in the largest cities. In New York, for example, day campers take swimming lessons in indoor pools and enjoy overnight camping experiences on apartment building roofs. More than 100,000 kids play softball, kickball, make clay pots and do most of the activities that kids traditionally do at camp.

Specialized Day Camps

Many of the programs offered by specialized residential camps can form the basis for specialized day camps as well. There are scores of computer day camps operating around the country, for example, and about a third of all residential computer camps offer daytime programs too.

Even where location doesn't play a major part in the decision, day camps are preferred by many parents for specialized types of programs. They're cheaper, of course, and for younger children, or children who may not be emotionally ready for an extended stay away from home, they seem made to order.

Starting Your Own Day Camp

After running a day camp in Vail, Colorado for four years, Colleen Corcoran wrote a book on the subject. Hiring the right staff is one of the points she emphasizes, and one summer she "imported" almost her entire staff from the University of Wisconsin, where she was studying at the time. Traits to look for, she says, include enthusiasm, experience, love of kids, and consistent dedication to work.

As in any business, you'll want to check out your market. "You've got to decide who you're going to sell to, how to get to them and what they can afford," Corcoran says. Her market was clearly made up of both tourists and locals. She went to the local newspaper, and her camp was written up in an article, and she also passed brochures out all over the small mountain town. Business took off.

When establishing her program, Corcoran was careful to check the local school schedules. "Make sure you're ready to go when school is out. Parents need to plug their kids into programs right away," she notes.

In setting your rates, you'll need to find out what the market will bear by checking the rates of similar programs in your area. Richard Brown charged $40 a week per child. Lynn Walker's Trojan Ranch charges twice that for its day-camp program, and in New York City fees range up to $100 a week or more.

Children from low-income families may qualify for subsidies through federal programs. While you're on the phone finding out about qualifications for these programs, you'll also want to find out about licensing requirements in your town. Some require day-care, day-camp or nursery licenses, and you should also check into any applicable state requirements. You may be required to buy specified types and amounts of insurance coverage and follow certain safety and sanitation procedures.

As with operating a day-care center, it's a good idea to have your policies regarding payment, illness, and emergencies written out to help avoid disputes with parents. A written daily schedule is also a good idea. It's only natural for parents to want to know what their offspring will be up to all day.

Before your camp opens, set aside some time to gather your staff together and discuss your philosophy, goals, and expectations for the program. Get their ideas and encourage them to interact and participate in the planning. You're going to be working as a team, and by showing them that you value their participation, they'll be more likely to care about the quality of work they do for you. In-service training should be continued throughout the season, and an evaluation of you, your program, and staff can help in putting together an improved program for the following season.

While planning your program, call the Chamber of Commerce and daily newspapers to see what events are planned in your community while camp is in session. Community events can be great excuses for field trips, and you may want to base craft activities and discussions on them as well.

Try to arrange at least one field trip out of town, even if it's just to go for a walk through a farmer's field. Invite a local expert on birds, wildlife, or botany, and an ordinary field can be transformed into a magical secret world teeming with life.

The American Camping Association has standards for day camps as well as residential camps. Your program should be located close enough to your campers that no more than one hour of travel will be required (one way). Provisions must be made for safe storage of supplies and equipment, and you must have shelter during bad weather. Finally, the ACA wants you to notify parents of any campers who are absent without explanation.

For the men and women who direct camps, it's an enriching and rewarding experience. As Don Cheeley puts it, "On the one hand, you're running a resort, handling food, maintenance, vehicles, sewage, water, equipment, housing. On the other hand, there's the personal satisfaction of being outdoors, of dealing with young people and having an impact on how they treat nature, of teaching them skills."

Wouldn't you love to start a camp for kids?

Chapter 6
Rags to Riches
In Kids' Clothes

Chris Scarlett was a 32-year-old devoted aunt when she began making clothes for her two nieces. With the encouragement of friends, "I took some things I had made into a Minneapolis shop, and I came out with an order." Six years later her sales hit $150,000, and she had representatives in Chicago, New York, San Francisco and Dallas marketing her "Scarlett Rabbitt" label.

Likewise, Carolyn Martin, now 50, didn't really plan to make a business out of silk-screening t-shirts for small children. "Being an artist is my real life," she says. But as a newly divorced parent with kids to support, she decided to try her hand at creating "nice things" for children. She says she's not quite sure what her gross sales were last year, but thinks they were "something upward of $65,000" — and two-thirds of that is profit.

Finally, Kathryn Conover became aware of the lack

of reasonably priced, high-quality clothing for children when her daughter was born in 1976. "Fine fabrics and classic design that fit my budget just didn't exist," she said. So she made clothing for Sophie and sold her work on the side to local shops. A few years later — with revenues approaching $1 million annually — she sold her business to a dress manufacturer in New York.

When it comes to children's clothes, style is back in style. Miniature Izod alligators, diminutive Diors, cute little Calvin Kleins — even tiny tuxedos — are to be found in nurseries across the country today.

According to the U.S. Dept. of Labor Statistics, 17 percent of the child-rearing budget of a moderate income family of four goes to clothes. The percentage must rise with income, though. In *The Ultimate Baby Catalog* Michele Igrassia Haber and Barbara Kantrowitz assemble a droolable collection of musts for the baby who has everything, including 6-month coats for $700, pram bags at $60 and made-to-order silk dresses with ruffles, lace, velvet, embroidery — whatever your heart desires — for up to $325.

Can you really compete with giant manufacturers like Calvin Klein, though? If you can combine good design, bright colors, high-quality fabric and good construction, the answer is yes. As children's boutique owner Karen Weinman puts it, "I'll buy a piece of clothing if it's something that definitely can't be mass-produced by a manufacturer. But it has to be contemporary and up-to-the-minute."

In today's market, "contemporary" often means fun. Today's on-the-go parents want more than just strong fabrics they can throw in the washing machine. They want bright, bold, stimulating colors. Designs that make even stodgy old Grandpa laugh. Dancing elephants. Gaily blowing balloons. Sweet lace collars. Embroidered diaper covers and tiny jogging suits.

PROFILES OF SUCCESS

The market for distinctive juvenile clothing is expected to continue growing for years to come. Estimates vary — with some projections as high as 10 percent a year — but most would agree that kid's clothing is an exciting, burgeoning industry.

It's a field that lends itself to numerous marketing approaches, too.

Designer T-Shirts

To begin her business, Carolyn Martin sold her house, moved to Washington, D.C. and put everything she had into Ami-shirts. "I decided to go for it," she recalls. "The rewards of answering to yourself rather than working for a corporation are much greater — if you can live up to your own convictions." Martin, who had previously worked as an art teacher, knew she could have gotten a job for someone as an art director but she was determined to produce high-quality, imaginative clothing for children. Money was an important consideration, too. "I was divorced and bringing up four children alone, so it was imperative that I had to earn more money than a teacher makes.''

Martin's business, Ami-shirts, specializes in charming silk-screened designs for little boys and girls on white, all-cotton t-shirts with nonleaded inks in bright primary colors. "We feel each shirt is a work of art, carefully designed and printed," Martin says. She is careful about copyrighting all of her designs but feels that, so far at least, competition has not been much of a problem.

For infants, she has a selection of 14 different messages, from "Hello, World" to "Brand New" and "Little Treasure." Some of the toddler shirts read "Petite Catastrophe," "We are the World," and "I am a Big Brother." Pictures of dolphins, numbers, letters, cats and other images are printed in five bright and beautiful colors.

"It's a lot of work, but when the final color goes on, we know it's been worth it," she says. Prices range from $7 to $12 for toddler long-sleeved shirts.

About half of Martin's business is handled through independent sales reps. She services the other half of her retail accounts herself. "I started doing big mailings to retailers and, believe it or not, stores would order sight unseen just from my mailings. You have to pack a little wallop into your brochure," she says. Because of her background in art, she is able to do all of the photography, design, and layout of her promotional materials herself.

Martin also teaches a course on small business at American University and is a consultant to other small businesses. She sometimes wonders if launching her business would have been easier if she had had a partner. "Having a partner might have meant more flexibility. If you trust each other and are good together, two heads are probably better than one," she says.

With or without a partner, Martin likes the idea of having a business at home. "It's good to be close to your children by working at home — if you can stand them and not look at all the dirt that needs sweeping up in the house. It's good for you, your income, and your children because they know that Mommy is not just a house cleaner and cook."

Martin's daughter, now 25, evidently learned the lessons well. Martin hopes to pass the business on to her when she retires and opens a studio in New York.

For the immediate future, she is changing the direction of her business slightly. Drying her hands in the kitchen one day, "It just came to me that European combination dishtowels, made of linen and cotton, would be a lovely, soft fabric for children's clothing." So with 500 yards of the stuff unrolled in her living room — and 12,000 more on order, she developed a new, "very European" line of clothing: baggier, more covered-up, with longer skirts, stockings, and more layers.

A strong advocate of quality, Martin is equally adamant about minimizing overhead. "Keep your costs as low as you possibly can except for the final product and then keep your costs as high as you possibly can. In other words put all your money into what the customer receives."

Martin feels children's clothing offers a great deal of opportunity now. "The competition just isn't there yet. Children's wear is a wonderful field because it's just so bad that there's all kinds of room for improvement in every direction . . .I mean there's *so* much room for improvement of children's wear in this country."

Personalized Labels

"It started as a fluke," says Chris Scarlett of her Scarlett Rabbitt label. Now primarily found in children's specialty shops, her clothes use ginghams, stripes, and calicos for quilted overalls and matching jumpers with hand-sewn appliques.

She filled her first order for three dozen halters in three different sizes after transforming her dining room into a factory. When she delivered the halters, the shop owner asked to see her fall line. Scarlett replied, "What's a fall line?"

It didn't take Scarlett long to find out what a fall line is, and before long she hired local seamstresses to sew in their homes, along with an assistant designer and several part-time employees. "I never dreamed that it would become so big," she said.

As orders came in from other local stores, she put all her profits back into the business, soon hiring sales representatives in Chicago, New York, San Francisco, and Dallas.

"Having your own business sounds glamorous, but it's hard work" she says. Like Martin, she began with too little capital, so she deliberately slowed her rate of growth "because it takes so much money to grow so fast."

A Multi-faceted Business

Jane Vohs, an art teacher and weaver, went into the children's clothing business after the birth of her second daughter. Intent on staying home with the kids, she was just as determined to keep her life interesting and her art career active.

Now, says Vohs with a laugh, business may be a little too interesting at times.

Vohs Unlimited got its start when Jane approached a local artisans' cooperative with her weaving. They had plenty of weavers, but they did need seamstresses, so Jane obliged. Soon she began to sell appliqued children's clothing and today she and a number of home sewers produce adorable aprons complete with teddy bears, ducks and pockets for scissors, crayons, paper, and glue.

Vohs markets her products through sales representatives. The reps take a commission of 10 to 20 percent, depending on their reputation and the product, but as Vohs points out, "you don't pay anything unless they generate sales for you." She also markets her wares at craft fairs.

For her line of specialty, quality items, Vohs found that mass retailing was not the way to go. "Small manufacturers can't get price breaks on fabric and supplies," she explains. Because of high material costs, her profit margin is too small to retail through outlets like big department stores. But selling through specialty shops, children's boutiques, and craft fairs allows her to charge enough to make a good profit.

Every marketing approach has its problems, of course. Most of the better children's stores do their buying in New York, for example, totally by-passing small manufacturers who, like Vohs, live and work in other parts of the country. "They figure everything will be in New York and if it's not there, it's not worth buying anyway," Vohs says.

There is another obstacle small manufacturers face: Big fabric suppliers don't like dealing with small orders — and surprisingly, some don't like dealing in cash. "I called up companies who wouldn't even accept a cashier's check for $500; they won't deal with you if you're not going to take out $20,000 in credit in a year. That's not how their books are set up." Other companies won't sell just one bolt of fabric, so Vohs has ended up with five when she really only needed half of one. She buys zippers by the hundreds, plastic eyes by the thousands, velcro and ribbon by the spools. "If the product wanes, or if you get tired of making it, you're stuck," she says.

Vohs considers quality control to be one of her hardest jobs. Occasionally she has to tell a sewer to re-do a job, and it's difficult for her to make that kind of assertion. "My husband says that if I were bigger I could hire someone to do that," she says.

There is also a certain amount of sexual discrimination Vohs has to deal with. There have been times when she has called to order fabric and the manufacturer on the other end won't deal with her, but when her husband calls, "He gets what he wants." At other times, the supplier has asked if her husband will make good on her debts, or they'll bill him, even though Vohs Unlimited is in her name. "He certainly is emotionally involved in my company, but he has zero to do with it," she says.

Cute little aprons aren't the only iron Vohs has in the fire. She also gets samples of children's clothing from manufacturers' reps and sells them from her home. Manufacturers send their new lines to their reps every season. After the reps have sold the line, they may buy the samples and re-sell them to sample shops or to people like Vohs, who then sell them at wholesale, plus one-third.

Competition for the samples is stiff, according to Vohs. Some reps don't want to break up the line, preferring to sell the whole bundle together. For a famous name like Izod or OP, the price can be substantial.

Has her company been financially successful? About 30 to 40 percent of her gross sales is profit, she says, and "To people who look at my books, it looks pretty good."

GUIDELINES FOR SUCCESS

Distinctive juvenile clothing is a fast growing, exciting market today. Retailers say that parents are opting for knits, natural fabrics, and "a total look" that includes accessories — right down to the shoes and socks. If you've got designs of your own you'd like to test market, here are a few things to consider.

- Avoid constricting elastic bands at the arms or ankles.

- Keep seams soft — not scratchy.

- Avoid metal zippers that can pinch a child's skin.

- Use machine-washable and driable fabrics that won't fade.

- Make sure your designs are easy to put on and take off a squirming baby or over-tired six-year-old.

- For baby clothes, parents prefer accessible diaper areas (in other words, easily opened crotches).

- Sweaters for young children should be tightly knit so fingers don't poke through.

- Pants for toddlers need to be especially strong to survive all that crawling and rolling, yet soft enough to prevent knee burns.

Children's outerwear involves additional considerations. Some suggestions include:

- Generous hoods keep baby dry and warm and aren't lost as easily as hats.

- Jackets should be long enough to reach below the

waist for better protection against the cold.

• Snowsuits for infants need closed hands and feet.

• Snowsuits for toddlers and older children should taper at the ankle to keep snow intake at a minimum.

• Plastic zippers are easier for young children to manipulate than buttons.

• Outer garments should be completely machine-washable.

OTHER OPPORTUNITIES IN KID'S CLOTHES

When most people think about opportunities in the children's clothing business the first thing they think of is a retail shop. There are, indeed, opportunities in retailing — opportunities in both new and used children's clothing.

Secondhand But Not Second Quality

Resale shops buy and sell previously owned children's clothing and accessories. Most of these shops accept items on consignment, paying the consignor 40 to 60 percent of the price actually received when the item sells. Some resale shops will also pay cash outright for clothes.

Clothing accepted for resale must be clean, pressed,

in good condition and in style. At most stores, it must also be appropriate for the season.

When clothing is accepted on consignment, a contract with the consignor is signed stipulating how long the agreement will last, what happens to the clothes after the deadline and what percentage of the receipts goes to each party. Clothes will typically hang in a shop for 90 days, and some stores offer them at a reduced price after 30 to 60 days. If they are not picked up by the deadline, they often will be donated to charity.

Some resale shops specialize in either large or small sizes, whereas others carry a broad selection of items including furnishings, scout and school uniforms, toys, accessories, and even maternity clothes. Often shops offer a request list for customers who want to be called when certain items come in, and it's not uncommon for shops to offer amenities such as community bulletin boards and play areas to keep children happy while their mothers are looking for bargains.

Operating on a consignment basis dramatically reduces the amount of capital required to go into business, but consignment usually does require more bookkeeping than regular retail operations. It took Dana Willenberg and her mother about six months to get their books "where we want them" for their Michigan resale shop. Every item has to be recorded and tagged when it comes in, and records have to be kept for each consignor as well. When the item is sold, is reduced or expires, the records must be updated.

Willenberg owns the Children's Exchange in her town. Started in Newburyport, Mass., by Karen Lynch,

there are now about 50 Children's Exchanges across the
country now. Lynch sells an operating manual with
detailed instructions on opening and operating such a
shop, including information on finding investment
money, choosing a location, designing a floor plan, buying and selling, pricing, what to buy and what to avoid,
advertising, accounting and bookkeeping. (see Appen-
dix A for ordering information).

"The financial rewards in this business are
exciting," says Lynch, who, by the way, does not advocate operating on a consignment basis. A Children's
Exchange in Michigan reportedly sold $1,200 worth of
clothing, equipment, and toys during its first day of
business, and Paulette Woodhatch took in almost
$1,000 the day her shop opened in Louisiana.

The Importance of Research

A big part of Linda Rinehart's "Childish Things"
shop is custom-made Halloween costumes created by a
local theater costumer. Hand-made for children and
adults, they make October Rinehart's best month.

She has so many people coming in some days, "I
don't know what I'd do if one more walked in." And
most of the people who bring clothes in to sell turn right
around and buy clothes while they're there.

For both Willenberg and Rinehart, opening the
business took months of preparation. Rinehart recommends doing extensive research. She talked to the Small
Business Administration and the Chamber of Commerce, and wrote people with similar shops in other

towns. She also visited consignment shops whenever she traveled. Then she sat down to figure out how much it would cost to open the business. "We overestimated almost everything," she says, which worked out fine, because the one thing they didn't overestimate — the cost of signs for the store — was about twice as much as they expected. She and a partner, who has since sold out, each took out loans for $6,000 to launch the business. An artist was hired to design a logo, and classified ads were placed to encourage people to bring in used clothing. To advertise the shop, Rinehart had kids from her church pass out fliers in various neighborhoods, paying them two cents a copy.

Now Rinehart has doubled her space and is trying direct-mail advertising. Her advice for others interested in starting a similar business: "Be prepared to work. It's a challenge to try, but you have to be committed. This is 50 hours a week plus. Money is important, but it takes time to build your business.

RETAILING NEW CLOTHES

For Barbara Harris, running a store is a lot like raising a child. "It's a lot of work at the beginning, but it gets better as you grow up together," she says with one of her frequent laughs.

Harris opened My New Friends four years ago when her business outgrew her home. She had been making "Catch Your Quackers" high chair mats since the birth of her "particularly messy" daughter, and was selling them to both wholesale and mail-order markets out of her home. The house got a little cluttered; "in fact, my husband suggested that I'd better take my business elsewhere," she recalls.

As she soon learned, moving her business out of her home and into a shop meant increased respect from customers but also the need for more permanent and prominent signs and attractive displays. Although the new location created its own share of problems, she would no longer be interrupted by burning casseroles — or sudden changes in residential zoning districts.

Since making the move, Harris' main problem has been landlords. In four years, she's operated out of three locations. "You can't realize how much rent obstructs your profit," she says. "You're at the mercy of your landlord." She was evicted from her first location because a high-rise was planned (it has yet to be built). The second landlord evicted her when he sold the building.

In every location Harris has moved into a low-rent area, developed a "cute" shop and attracted other businesses which opened shops nearby. Unfortunately, her landlords have tended to reward her efforts at upgrading her location by doubling her rent.

When Jeanette Ouazanan and her husband opened their shop, Les Enfants, they also chose a less-than-ideal location. With several very well known, posh restaurants in the area, "it wasn't barren," she says. "But still, most people said we were crazy. It wasn't Rodeo Drive in Beverly Hills." It's still not, but today their Melrose Avenue location is one of Los Angeles's fashionable shopping areas, and Ouazanan is proud of her success and proud that "we've been in the same location for five years."

What does it cost to open a children's wear shop? The figure varies tremendously, of course, but Harris spent money earned from her mat business — between $7,000 and $9,000 — to open her store. Carpeting (about $1,000) and painting were initial major expenses, along with the required first and last months' rent. She was able to keep inventory costs down by contacting local artists and arranging for them to place mobiles and children's accessories in the shop on consignment. "That's our biggest draw now," she says. The store's stock includes her own mats, jingle bracelet and Tender Knees pads for crawlers, as well as items produced by local craftspeople. She specializes in the mid-range of children's clothing and shower gifts for kids up to age 6.

Now Harris' inventory of children's clothing has increased to about $30,000, and in the last year her revenues have doubled. She is justifiably proud of having increased the size of her inventory without borrowing money, and she's proud of what she's learned through first-hand experience. "I learned to start paying my bills on time, a little bit at a time, to placate the manufacturers. I was completely naive in the beginning, but that may have worked to my advantage. I learned by doing."

Unlike My New Friends, Les Enfants is targeted to the upper-middle- to high-class market. Considering the shop's location in Los Angeles, that means "a lot of entertainers," Jeanette says. The store is known for its distinctive and colorful handmade clothing, as well as its

European imports.

It was the imported clothes that formed the inspiration for the store in the first place. When the Ouazanans' baby was born, Jeanette's French in-laws sent beautiful baby clothes. Jeanette joked that her husband should open a store, but he took her idea seriously, found the location and went to Paris to buy inventory.

As a result, "We were the first boutique with imported clothing for children," Jeanette says.

The success of Les Enfants, Jeanette believes, is based on a clear perception of the store's purpose and clientele. "You have to have a good idea about what you want to carry. If you're too easily swayed by what your friends want you to carry, it can be a mess. Establish in your head the look you want — and go for it," she advises. Once you have the initial concept in mind, "look at everything in the markets." Jeanette didn't pass by homemade goods, for example. Today she still finds hand-painted diaper sets and hand-appliqued sweaters popular.

Harris attributes part of her success to the role she has come to play in the Santa Monica community. "We're just a nice, personable store," she says. "We build up a camaraderie with our customers," most of whom she knows personally. The shop will soon be offering classes in cardiopulmonary resuscitation and talks by social workers and a pediatrician. Harris' advertising budget has always been small; by bringing people into the shop for talks or puppet shows, she hopes to reinforce the role of her shop as a community resource and build her clientele.

Jeanette Ouazanan's clientele was almost built-in from the beginning. When the shop first opened, she shared the space with her husband, a successful hairdresser. "I fed off his clientele," she recalls. Word soon spread about her shop, and in two years she took over the entire space.

As Jeanette discovered, a good shop location is more than a matter of cheap rent. Small shops depend on the customers attracted to nearby department stores and other businesses in the area. Of course, department stores may offer lower prices than a specialty boutique, but your marketing should emphasize your personal service and the high quality of your merchandise. You should try to find a location that benefits from the flow of customers generated by nearby stores without allowing the competition to have an adverse effect.

"Word of mouth is still my best advertising," Jeanette says. Even after five years, "I don't really know all that I should about PR." She does know that advertising in the *Los Angeles Times* and on local morning television talk shows works well for her. And postcards advising her customers about sales and new merchandise have paid off, too. If you're just starting out, she suggests searching out all the papers, magazines and other media in your area. Find out what advertising costs for different media and determine what you can afford. Then just start experimenting.

Like so many women in business, Ouazanan and Harris are also mothers. For Harris, family obligations always take priority over business. She leaves the shop without exception every day at 2 p.m. to pick up her children at school, and when her daughter was seriously ill not long ago, she completely ignored the store.

Jeanette points out that good day care may be a business woman's best investment. "You must have peace of mind to work," she points out. Otherwise both your business and your family's well-being are likely to suffer.

Setting Up Shop

To be successful, a children's wear shop must be attractive to both children and parents. Jeanette Ouazanan attributes a major part of her shop's success to appearance — it's a "cute little gingerbread house," she says.

An attractive shop means good organization and care: shiny windows and mirrors, vacuumed carpets, clean tile floors, and orderly, properly arranged merchandise. Les Enfants, for example, displays goods for boys and girls in three distinct areas: one for infants, another for clothing sizes 2 to 4 and a smaller section for sizes 5 to 8.

Any shop, no matter how small, needs a place to receive, tag, and prepare in-coming merchandise for sale. You'll need a desk for writing orders, shelves for supplies, hanging rods and storage boxes. You'll also need a stock room or rack for reserve merchandise and you'll need procedures for receiving merchandise.

You should plan your shop so as to maximize convenience to both your sales people and your customers. Try to make your merchandise easy to process and easy to find once it's on the floor. Use lighting, rugs, tile, paint, and wallpaper to create an atmosphere of ease and comfort and to show your merchandise at its best advantage. Many shops use wall racks and permanent shelves for regularly priced merchandise, with floor racks highlighting special items which are new or on sale.

Buying can be an intimidating chore for new shop-keepers. "The key is to look — look at everything," says Ouazanan. "Then let your own good taste be your guide." When you open, you don't want too few items because it will look like you have a skimpy selection. Too large an inventory, on the other hand, will tie up too much capital, place a strain on your floor space and unnecessarily increase your risk. Experienced retailers advise buying just enough merchandise for your first 90 days.

Chapter 7
Unexpected Opportunities
In Kids' Accessories

"Our industry is experiencing a growth rate like we've never seen."
— Bill MacMillan, executive director
Juvenile Products Manufacturing Association

"Accessories" is a catch-all term that applies to all types of kids' gear other than toys and clothing. It includes such diverse products as crib linens, bibs, children's artwork and furniture — and it's an industry that is growing at least 14 percent a year.

If you have an idea for a product that might simplify or beautify or otherwise enhance the lives of children (and, in the process, of Moms and Dads), give some serious thought to transforming your idea into a business. The kids' accessories market is big (over $1.15 billion), it's growing, and there's no question that good opportunities exist for imaginative new products.

Success stories are not hard to find.

The Stuff of Dreams

Pansy Ellen Essman grew up on a farm and only had an eighth grade education, but she was always a creative person. When her back ached from bathing her squirming granddaughter in an adult-sized tub, she promptly came up with a solution to the problem. It came to her in a dream one night — an idea for a polyurethane "bath aid" which is a big piece of sponge scooped out to hold a wiggly, wet baby safely in place in a slippery tub or sink.

Using scrap materials, Essman was able to design and build equipment to produce the bath aids. She made a few "on the side" and then quit her factory job. With no money and no marketing knowledge, she struggled for a year. Finally, her family put up $30,000 to help her produce 1,000 of her bath aids. Even then the road was far from easy.

"As an entrepreneur, you always hear, 'Your idea is no good,' " Pansy Ellen says. "Most people thought my product wouldn't go, that it looked too much like a mummy case and that it would harbor bacteria." Nevertheless, she was determined to make it succeed, and she was able to place a few at local children's shops on a consignment basis. They sold, and more orders followed.

Encouraged, Pansy Ellen decided to wing it. With the help of her American Express card, she showed her product at a juvenile trade show in New York. "It was do or die. Either I brought home orders, or I'd be bankrupt when I got home," she now says with a laugh. Impressed both by her unusual product and her perseverance, about a dozen sales reps took on her bath aids. And growth, inevitably, followed.

Today Pansy Ellen has 45 employees manufacturing the bath aid and an expanding line of other juvenile products: lamps, a hook-on canvas chair, baby food organizers, a nursery jar set and a bentwood replica of a 100-year-old high chair. Last year her company grossed close to $5 million, and she has been recognized by the International Council of Small Business Management and Development for her success.

Pansy Ellen has some good advice for would-be juvenile marketers: "If you think your product is going to really fill a need, by all means, go ahead and do it. Don't listen to the people who say it can't be done," she urges. "Don't let them get you down."

Lack of money shouldn't keep you from trying, either, according to Pansy Ellen. "I went without food to keep going," she recalls. With a laugh she adds, "I'd go to my sisters' to eat. I never told them why I always came at meal time."

Sewing Up Success

Nancy Garwood didn't like placing her baby on a hot, sticky plastic car seat. Yet with more and more publicity being given to the dangers of allowing unrestrained children to ride in cars, there seemed to be little choice.

Taking the initiative, Nancy designed and sewed a quilted cotton cover to fit over her baby's safety seat. Soon she was creating car seat covers for admiring friends who couldn't sew. Encouraged by their enthusiasm, she showed samples to a local infant furnishings store, and the owner agreed to sell them. Before long, Nancy was selling about four dozen a week.

At first, Garwood hired neighbors to sew for her. Her own sewing machine could make buttonholes big enough to accommodate the chair safety straps but her neighbors' machines couldn't, so for awhile she had to make all the buttonholes — up to 350 a week. Later she located a contractor in Baltimore who began doing her sewing for her.

As the first company to introduce a car seat cover to the market, Garwood's timing was excellent. In 1977 people were just realizing that car accidents are the biggest killer of children under 5, whereas today more than 40 states have passed legislation making the use of car seats mandatory.

There are now more than a dozen manufacturers of car seat covers, however, and Nancy is no longer the largest. Unfortunately she had no way to patent what is essentially a slip-cover. Because of the rapid increase in competition she encountered, Nancy advises anyone who wants to manufacture and market a product for children to plunge in — immediately.

In her own case, she had no business experience and now feels she was a little too cautious. "I had a hot item. I should have marketed it more widely right away and sought more capital to invest in it. I could have eliminated some of the competition I have now," she says.

Nevertheless, Nanci Industries is now selling products through some seventeen independent sales reps in Canada and Puerto Rico and throughout the U.S. In 1977 about 400 covers were sold at about $14 each; last year sales were close to $1 million, with an expanded line of covers for car seats, playpens, changing tables, and strollers.

One Moore Success Story

In the early 1960s Michael and Ann Moore served a term in the Peace Corps in French West Africa. When they returned home, one of the things they brought back with them was a great deal of respect for the emotional well-being of African children, a quality at least partly due to the close contact maintained between mother and child during the first years of life.

When Ann gave birth a few months after her return to the U.S., she tried to concoct a carrier similar to the ones in which African women toted their babies. Her mother, back home in Ohio, sewed a more secure version with one pouch positioned inside a larger pouch, both of which were zippered. Wide shoulder straps crisscrossed Ann's back, and a waistband kept her baby from swinging from side to side. The result was the first Snugli carrier, today sold — and soon to be manufactured — around the world. The Snugli line now includes diaper bags, lamb skins, portable beds and cassette tapes for relaxation before and during childbirth.

Initially Snuglis were sold through mail-order, particularly through childbirth and nursing organizations. A few stores, which Mike Moore describes as "Mom and Pop boutiques," became interested. Then department stores, catalog showrooms, and big chain stores wanted to get in on the act.

Snugli met this growing market by selling directly to retailers through its own reps. "We didn't go through distributors because we wanted control of distribution," Mike explains. In addition, use of outside distributors would have built increased costs into the end-price of the product.

Mike was working as program director for a philanthrophic foundation when Snugli began to take off. He quit his job, "and I found myself promptly out of my depth," he now says with a laugh. For help, he went to a lawyer for advice. "He sat me down and said, 'Get an accountant.' "

The Moores began producing the original Snugli with the help of home-sewers. Eventually some 150 home sewers were involved, and the line was broadened "to span the price range," from the top-of-the-line hand-crafted corduroy or seersucker carrier to a high-quality, but more affordable model.

Snugli will soon have three locations in metropolitan Denver and one in Japan. Plants in Denmark and Canada are also being established.

GETTING STARTED

Meg Hansson worked during school hours and at

night doing public relations and advertising for a friend's mountaineering equipment company until she and he hatched the idea for a kiddy carrier. Now retired as the president of Gerico, which manufactured some of the first front and back carriers for babies, Hansson has worked as a consultant to small business — and to U.S. presidents. She helped the Juvenile Product Manufacturing Association write its standards, and she is known as one of the top female executives in the U.S. today.

If you want to get started in the kids' accessories business, Hansson recommends first of all being open to information. "I'm a 55-gallon drum of miscellaneous information about topics like patents, legal requirements, safety, dealing with an accountant, lawyers, sales reps, imports and quotas," Hansson says. You need to know how your product will be made and how it will be marketed. "Question all the people dealing in children's goods in whatever area you're in," she advises.

Read about management. Learn to think ahead, "way ahead." Join professional groups, manufacturer's groups, business owners' groups. Talk to the Small Business Administration.

Go to every children's department and every children's store you can. "Look at everything out there," Hansson recommends. Talk to other manufacturers. See what they're selling. Examine how it's made and sold. "Chances are good that a company in your field knows almost every major improvement on their product," she says. There's probably a good reason why they haven't made the particular change you think will sell like hot cakes. Try to find out what their reason is.

Mike Moore also has advice to offer newcomers to the industry. First, "recognize your own limits and where you need help. Then get the best help available." He adds, "Never be afraid to ask for advice, but never accept advice without wondering how you might need to modify it in some way to apply to you." Mike strongly recommends hiring a good accountant — if only to set up proper record-keeping procedures, to help identify costs and to help price your products.

There are many things to consider in producing products for kids. Safety, versatility, convenience and appearance are some of the most important considerations.

Safety

As with toys and any other products for children, safety considerations must be paramount. The safety features your particular accessory will need will depend entirely on the product. In general, though, if you can think of a way to make your product safer to own and use, any added expense created by the safety feature will probably be justified. Parents today are willing to pay for quality in the products they buy for their children, and safety features are a very important part of quality.

Children's car seats are a case in point. "Twelve years ago parents bought a car seat to keep the children out of the parents' hair," says Bill MacMillan of the Juvenile Products Manufacturers' Association (JPMA).

Today, parents demand that those seats pass rigid safety tests. Consequently, the seats "cost ten times as much, and we're selling ten times as many," he says.

JPMA plays an important role in promoting safe children's accessories by establishing rigorous safety standards and certifying products which meet those standards.

Versatility

With more and more people moving into town-houses, condominiums and other housing options with limited living space, versatility has become extremely important in children's accessories. If you can find a way to make your product multi-functional yet compact, you'll have a built-in marketing advantage.

Some of the products currently on the market admirably demonstrate this type of versatility:

- a crib that converts into a youth bed, both with drawers,

- a hexagonal crib with storage space below,

- a high chair which converts into a youth chair,

- a dresser which doubles as a changing table,

- a baby-sized sleeping bag with a pouch at the feet for diaper storage,

Convenience

Convenience has always been an important selling point, but with increasing numbers of two-career couples and single-parent households the value of convenience has reached an all-time high. Parents want that storage space for diapers in the sleeping bag because it means less to carry. The convertible high chair can save shopping for a new seat when Baby outgrows the old one.

Vinyl wallpaper for the kid's room makes cleaning easier. Light switch extensions allow little people to turn the lights on — and hopefully off — at their own whim. Holders for changing table necessities like cotton balls, lotions, and thermometers sell well, as do organizers for books, crayons, and art supplies. Anything that makes raising kids easier, simpler, and less time-consuming has definite market potential today.

Appearance

Finally, parents want accessories that add beauty to Baby's room and the home in general. Appliqued, embroidered or quilted comforters, blankets, baby carriers, and seat liners are growing in popularity. Soft sculpture wall hangings, hand-carved ornaments, and music boxes in all shapes and sizes find a ready market today.

Take a look at products on the market that are functional but visibly unappealing and ask yourself how you can improve on them. Sometimes a more beautiful appearance is all that's required to turn an old idea into a highly successful new product.

A FEW BIG SELLERS

The range of products included in the children's accessories field is extremely broad, but some of the big sellers on the market today include cradles, storage units, linens and artwork.

Cradles

Cradles are experiencing renewed popularity today, at least partly because a cradle at the foot of the parent's bed provides a nice compromise between the family bed concept and the feelings of isolation that an infant can experience if placed in another room. As always, the rocking motion of a cradle seems to have a calming effect on fussy babies and helps them ease into sleep. Made of maple, cherry, walnut, oak — even brass or gold plate — cradles range from about $75 to $2,000.

Handmade cribs are being successfully marketed today, too. Some come with built-in drawers while others are reproductions of classic designs from the past.

Safety requirements for both cribs and cradles are stringent and should be carefully researched.

Storage Units

Storage units and toy boxes are growing in popularity as the size of our houses shrinks and the amount of kids' gear we buy grows. Handmade toy boxes, designed for contemporary whimsy or classic simplicity, are always a good possibility. Be sure to consider safety requirements, though — you'll want to install a mechanism to keep the lid from suddenly dropping on a small head or hand. Big block boxes not only are useful for storage, they're also handy for hide-and-go seek if the boxes are big enough and the children small enough. Put castors on the bottom and you've got an instant choo-choo train. When the child outgrows the train, the boxes can provide needed storage for the elementary school years.

Play Areas

Play areas, with an emphasis on custom design, always seem to be good sellers. The trick is to develop imaginative, fun, yet safe environments that incorporate your client's trees, fences, patio or other structures.

If you can find ways to put recycled materials to creative use, you can save money and increase your profits. You can create an impressive obstacle course, for example, from old 55-gallon drums, railroad ties, tractor tires and cargo netting. Remember to check with local building codes before adding playhouses or treehouses.

Softgoods

In the last five years linens have grown to the point where they account for 15 percent of all juvenile product sales, according to an article in *The New York Times*. When you consider some of the prices involved, it's not hard to see why. Tiny terry towels with a corner pocket for Baby's head sell for up to $30, a baby bath towel set retails for up to $70 and sheets with hand-sewn lace sell for over $100.

California retailer Bernard Zwick says that ten years ago manufacturers didn't offer much for kids beyond the white canopy you saw here and there — but today "It's so style-oriented that we buy every quarter for fashion."

Artwork

Finally, all types of artwork for Baby's room are steadily growing in popularity. Parents today realize that, in addition to being beautiful, room decorations stimulate their baby's mind and can be an aid to development. Nursery walls should be whimsical, colorful and fun. There's a ready market for all types of wall hangings, and mobiles and wind chimes are also popular today.

TO SUM UP

"I've been in this industry about fourteen years," says Bill MacMillan. "Ten years ago, the industry's products were sold primarily on price. Today, price is only one of four or five considerations, and it is not the chief one." Safety, style, convenience, and durability are equally important to today's busy but conscientious parents.

With those criteria in mind, your accessory idea

could well take off and carry you to success. As Margaret Hansson says, there is always room for a new style, "a new, bright idea."

Chapter 8
The "Write" Stuff
(and related opportunities)

Now 60, Ouida Sebestyen started writing when she was 20 and finally turned to children's literature after "I'd tried everything else: novels, plays, true confessions, poetry." Two years ago she sent a story to Atlantic-Little Brown to see if the publisher be interested in it as a book (it had been published as a story fourteen years earlier in *Ingenue*). They were. After four unsold novels, an unsold play and forty-seven unpublished short stories, Sebestyen's "Words by Heart" won an American Book Award and bought her and her son a new house.

"I felt like Cinderella," Sebestyen recalls.

If your life is "a natural love affair with literature," as one writer phrased it, you may be able to create your own Cinderella story by writing for the children's market. As Jane Fitz-Randolph, author of

Writing for Children and Teens, says, "It's a profession where there's a lot of room at the top."

Publishers today are looking for good juvenile literature. As bookstores increase the size of their children's departments, publishers are spending more on advertising, putting more authors on tour and prodding their sales forces to push juvenile titles more aggressively. The market for educational materials and computer software is showing explosive growth. "It's a good time to come on board," says Terry Morris, a nationally known author.

Writing, like tying your shoelaces, tennis and trigonometry, is a skill that is learned. All it takes is practice. Almost everyday.

You may not write a classic, but who knows? You may. With imagination, research, hard work and chutzpah — that requirement for success in any type of self-employment — the world of children's writing may provide the opportunity you're looking for, whether your interest is in fiction, nonfiction, or related areas like scriptwriting, producing educational aids, or illustration.

WRITING

The Importance of Quality

Children's literature has undergone profound changes since the first "chap books" and dime novels aimed at children appeared on the market. Without question, the changes have been for the better.

Today, "the best reading in the library is in the children's room," as Kathleen Phillips, who wrote a few of them, puts it. "Children won't read on if they don't like the first page," she explains. Many people would agree. Author Loyd Alexander says, "Children's books are written to be read; adult books are written to be talked about at cocktail parties." Although deceptively simple in appearance, successful children's books tend to be carefully researched, accurate, and extremely well written.

What does "well written" mean when applied to children's literature? It means colorful nouns, vivid verbs and similies, lively dialogue, lots of antecdotes — in other words, "forceful, picture-making language," as Phillips says. The best children's writing has simple, action-filled, sensual but straightforward prose, and a vocabulary suited to the reading level of the child for whom you're writing. It also has "hard words and concepts translated graphically in terms a child can understand," according to Elizabeth Hennefrund, a Washington, D.C. writer and former associate editor of *Ranger Rick's Nature Magazine*.

Whether funny, informative, wacky or whimsical, children's writing must capture and hold the young reader's interest. It should open doors into worlds beyond the child's immediate environment — even if it's about his own backyard.

Briefly, in good children's writing:

- the characters and action must catch and hold the reader's attention.

- the information should be lively, whether fact or fiction.

- it should speak to the child's interests.

- the language should be vivid, but also clear and simple.

- it should not talk down to the age at which it is targeted.

- it should not contribute to sex-role or racial stereotyping.

- fiction should move along briskly and there should be plenty of action.

- the child should be able to identify with the hero/heroine.

- adults, as well as children, should be able to enjoy the story.

- if nonfiction, the information must be clear, accurate and effectively presented.

Why is quality so important in children's writing? Through early books and stories, even the youngest baby being read to begins to appreciate the rhythm of language and the way words are used in sequence. This is a child's first exposure to the written word, and the wrong experience can mean his interest in reading will be delayed for years — perhaps even permanently.

Through reading, children learn to abstract ideas, to expand their horizons, to use their imaginations. They learn to create pictures in their minds, far beyond those on the printed page. They learn to plunge into deeper and deeper meanings as they mature and reread old favorites, and they learn to appreciate more subtle aspects of writing such as symbolism.

A good book enhances a child's life in many ways. A nature book can prepare him for a trip to the zoo or to Yellowstone National Park. A book about construction may increase his enjoyment of a walk downtown. A storybook will give a five-year-old new idioms with which to delight himself and his parents. Just ask any family whose child has been seen muttering to himself, "I do not like green eggs and ham!"

Perhaps most importantly, a good book will enhance and enrich communication within the family, providing an opportunity to sit and learn together about seashells or fairytales or holidays. It will be read and discussed and reread and discussed some more.

Market Research

As in so many other fields, the first order of business in becoming a children's writer is to survey the market.

Flip through the most current issue of *Writer's Market* in the reference room at the public library. You'll notice that most of the juvenile periodicals seem to be focused on topics like literature, health, nature and religion, although there are some general-interest children's publication, too. *Writer's Market* gives details on what each publication wants to buy, and the range includes articles, fiction, profiles, fantasy, drama, and poetry.

Now stroll over to the periodical department and read through as many of those magazines as you can. Look through the library's children's room next, and then survey what your local bookstores carry for children. What you are doing, of course, is finding out what is currently available for children. What is there an abundance of? What is missing? Notice plot development, characterization, how illustrations tie into the text.

Talk to educators, retailers, parents, and librarians to find out what kinds of new books they'd like to see. What do they admire that's already in print? Read it. Don't forget that, whatever it is you're selling in the juvenile market, adults buy things for kids (so they're the ones you have to sell).

Targeting Your Market

Writing, like toys and clothes, must be "age appropriate." The first step is to get to know your readers. If you want to know what kids want or need to read, spend time with them. Talk to kids about what they're learning or what they want to know. What do they love? What do they read over and over? What would they like to read about? Try to remember what you felt like, what you were interested in, when you were the age at which you're targeting your writing.

There's one other point that should be made about trying to be age appropriate. A key principle in characterization in children's stories and books is that kids read up, not down. This means that eleven-year-olds are likely to be interested in reading about thirteen-year-olds but they're very unlikely to want to read about nine-year-olds.

Here are some guidelines about who reads what when.

Infants

Some experts recommend that children as young as six months have books in the crib with them to chew and fondle, to give them a good first taste of reading, so to speak. First books must be sturdy. There isn't a big selection of books for this age, and most have brilliant colors and representational drawings of familiar objects like Mom, Dad, Baby, and dog.

By nine months an infant may be able to moo at the cow in her picture book. This age loves textured pages, cloth books, books to smell and feel.

One Year

This guy can turn the pages. He still wants dazzling colors, and now he's ready for more intricate drawings as long as it's nothing too abstract. Many one-year-olds are ready to hear a real story with a beginning, middle and end as long as the activity per page is minimal. He loves hearing about the rituals of his own life and loves listening to rhymes.

Pre-Schoolers

Two- and three-year-olds are active learners and seem to soak up what they read. They can hold books themselves now, and they're interested in true situations yet also enjoy a combination of reality and fantasy. Animal stories are still tops among pre-schoolers. Children seem to identify with animals, perhaps because they live more simply than people. Animals are uncritical and never give orders like some parents most kids could name. As one expert put it, animals are "a safe remove from reality."

As pre-schoolers grow older they look to books to explain the workings of the world: why there are clouds and how the moon gets up in the sky every night. By the age of four they love to laugh, and mixed-up, goofy language does the trick every time. Pop-up books are also a big hit at this age.

Five Years

Books that explain myths, legends, customs and cultures are good now, more explanations to answer the five-year-old's unceasing "why" and "how" questions. Other books encourage their penchant for make-believe, a more sophisticated way of pretending than they previously indulged in.

Early Elementary

By six, a child wants resource books about cooking, gardening, history, and people. It's time for easy readers as well.

Later Elementary

Nedda Nussbaum of Random House suggests that children of this age love "the odd, strange, amazing; record-holders (biggest, fastest, etc.) of all sorts." They want more facts, and that means resource books about everything: geography, sports, nature, history, you name it. They read for information as much as for entertainment, and their grasp of the topics they're interested in can be surprisingly sophisticated.

Generating Ideas

For some people, getting a good idea is the most difficult part of writing. For others, ideas seem to just drip off trees as they walk under them. Ideas are everywhere, but you may have to train yourself to see them. Without an idea there is no book — without an aim or focus, your project is just a hazy dream.

Finding an idea begins with your own interests, plus a healthy amount of poking and peeking around. Consultant, university teacher, and award-winning writer Karen O'Conner says, "Over the years I've become a kind of snoop, staying alert to the people and events closest to me. I jot down bits of dialogue, names, dates, stray facts that intrigue me, snappy titles — whatever the time. Then I play with these bits and pieces until something clicks. If an idea takes shape quickly, I continue working with it. If it's slow and frustrating, I put it down and go on to something else.''

Author and editor Barbara Shook Hazen adds, ''I have gotten my best ideas from eavesdropping, observation, woolgathering and, oddly, after working dog hard trying to think through a concept that won't work. Often something else pops up like a crocus and does work. It's as if, after a lot of effort, instinct takes over.''

Talking to teachers, kids and parents while surveying the market may provide you with enough workable ideas for the present. To ensure that you continue to come up with ideas, cultivate the habit of watching your friends and family with a critical eye. Notice what makes them laugh, what makes them grumpy, what predicaments they find themselves in and how they get out. Listen to kids playing across the street — and the kids in your kitchen. Ask teachers what funny or touching incidents they remember. Hang out at a playground, listen to kids in the library, visit a school or day-care center and really listen.

Everywhere you go, take a pencil and paper and take notes about what you see and hear. Even leave a notepad by your bed; how many times do you really remember the sudden inspiration that awakened you in the middle of the night?

Successful authors recommend writing classes, taken with a grain or so of salt. Some of them are excellent, but others are not really helpful. You can learn a lot simply by reading — and reading some more. And it can be a major help if you can get together with fellow writers to exchange ideas and encourage one another.

The following dos and don'ts, from editor Glen Evans and writers Kathleen Phillips and Ouida Sebestyen, lay out some general guidelines:

- Don't write down to your readers. Although average reading ability has declined in recent years, children are increasingly sophisticated because of television and other media. There's growing market interest in "high/low" books — high interest/low reading ability — as a result.

- Likewise, don't arbitrarily limit the themes you tackle. Today's kids deal with realities like two-family homes, divorce, and alcoholism in ways previous generations never dreamed of. There also is a growing market for books that address problems kids themselves face, like drugs, alcohol, and peer pressure.

- Do respect your readers. Strive to look at your work and the world through their eyes.

- Don't preach or over-moralize, even for a religious magazine.

- Do have the child protagonist be the main mover in your story.

- "Do be willing to give a year of your life — or however long it takes — to something, to be set on fire by that something," Sebestyen suggests, and adds,

- "Most importantly, don't ever, ever give up."

Getting to Work

Once you've got your idea clearly in mind you'll need to make a commitment. Writing is working — sitting down for however many hours you can give yourself each day and pounding away at those keys, thinking, searching for the right word, editing. It takes time.

It also takes research. It may be as simple as your careful observation of your neighbor's kids, around whom you are crafting a picture book. Or it may be detailed research into the life cycle of the giraffe. In any case, remember that you can always leave some facts out if you have too many, but you can never make up what you haven't yet learned. So overdo it. Strive for accuracy.

Finally, the moment can no longer be avoided. You've read every book in the library on your subject, your pencils are sharp and the paper is in the typewriter.

Well, just begin. If you can't think of a beginning, start wherever you can and proceed from there.

Many experienced writers warn against perfectionism in your first draft. Remember that the object of the first draft is simply to rough out your ideas; there'll be plenty of time for revisions and improvements later.

Try to relax and just let your ideas flow.

Once you've got some kind of rough draft, try to forget about it for awhile. Think about other things and your subconscious will come up with new insights, new approaches you can take to get around the parts you're having problems with.

Don't worry if your original idea takes completely new directions as you create more drafts. Just realize that your ideas are gradually becoming refined and that creativity often takes time and patience.

For picture books, most writers suggest actually creating a "dummy" (mock-up) of the book by cutting out paper and physically laying out the book. Then you can write the text as it will appear on each page with sketches and written ideas for the illustrations.

Picture book or sixth-grade novel, after the writing you'll need to edit your work. Have a dictionary at the ready, and make sure every word says what you want it to say. Read out loud to yourself as you work through your manuscript — you'll be amazed how much you can improve upon your work simply by listening to the words flow with a critical ear. Don't pretend that your words are sacred. Change, edit, and after sleeping on it some more, go back and read through it again. Read through everything at least three times before you type your final draft.

On the other hand, don't edit your work to death. Remember that you'll never get it absolutely, 100 percent perfect, and your editor will probably want to make some changes anyway. At some point, it's time to say "enough!" Package it up and ship it off, and try not to worry about it anymore.

Marketing

Most writers say an agent will not necessarily help you to sell a manuscript. If it's good and, according to your survey of the market, sellable, it will be considered by editors.

You may send either your completed manuscript or a query letter, depending on the preference of the publisher (*Writer's Market* will guide you here). If you only send a query, your letter will have to do all of your selling for you. Make it good. Grab the editor's attention with specific facts you have uncovered in your research that are brought out in your book, or provide a graphic summary of the plot. Be sure to tell the purpose of your manuscript and the age group for which it is intended.

If you're marketing a book manuscript, include a chapter outline and describe the kind of illustrations you would use. Be as persuasive as possible in describing its sales potential.

The editor will want to know how your book is better than the competition. *Books in Print* has information about other books available on your topic, and you can find it at your public library. You should be thoroughly familiar with your competition so you can tell your editor how your book is different and special.

Most children's writers recommend keeping your manuscript in the mail until it sells. "You have to be tough," says Kathleen Phillips. "You get an awful lot of rejection. You can't take it personally . . . ."

Kathleen met success late in life. She came from a family that enjoyed writing for amusement, so she wrote all her life, studied writing in college and even after college while she raised her family. "Yet the thought of publishing seemed presumptious," she says.

At the suggestion of a teacher, she submitted a story to the children's page of the *Christian Science Monitor*. It ran. Later she wrote adult essays for that paper, and while she was still raising her kids, she began selling her books.

Kathleen believes she was lucky to have a husband who brings home the bacon. "It takes a long time to get established. It helps to have an independent income," she says.

Looking Ahead

What will the future hold for children's writers?

What's certain is that the market for children's writing will not stay the same. Writers will have to be flexible in choosing the topics they cover and the approaches they take.

Some believe there will be more stress on visuals in juvenile publishing thanks to the influence of television and other media. Easy-to-read books will continue to be popular, along with more sophisticated topics for children. As national publishing houses become more concentrated and centralized, more regional publishers will step in, including regionally oriented publishers of children's books.

Realistic picture books, toy and game books should continue to sell well, and there continues to be unmet demand for light, contemporary fiction of about 120 to 150 pages for eight- to twelve-year-olds. There's a ready market for high interest books for teens who read at second or third grade level (and adults who are learning English as a second language).

Remember that the standards of good writing don't change. That's what makes a classic a classic, and with enough care, maybe you'll be the next writer of a classic.

SCRIPTWRITING

Juvenile script writers are needed to cover a vast array of subjects in a variety of media. Films, filmstrips, multimedia shows, video, records, screenplays, stage plays, and television are all reaching children today, and new media are continually being developed. *Writer's Market* says, for example, "The ever-increasing cable TV outlets should be good news for the writer." Children's theater is booming as well. In a Monticello, New York children's theater, a new play about teenage drug addicts and alcohol abusers reached nearly 50,000 youngsters its first year.

Admittedly, it's a world that's hard to break into. It helps to have a name for yourself, and one way to begin is to script for local radio or television stations or amateur theater. Enter competitions when you get the chance. Publishers and producers want to know that you have experience.

Good scriptwriting has a fresh narrative style with

creative use of dialogue, good organization, clarity, and originality. It is based on thorough research and has a liveliness and innovative style that comes through the drama.

Theater buffs will find listed in *Writer's Market* a number of theaters that are looking for new children's plays. As the Russian actor Stanislavski said, "Theater for children is not different from adult theater, only better." That's probably because it must be direct, clear, and enjoyable to adults as well as children. While entertaining plots are essential, good children's plays should also have strong characters with whom young people can easily identify. Many theaters want scripts that are technically simple, short plays, adaptations, or reader's theater pieces.

EDUCATIONAL AIDS

Seven years after Kathy Kolbe's business got its start on her ping pong table she was honored at the White House as one of the nation's outstanding small business people. Today, at age 44, she is head of the largest publishing company of educational aids for gifted students in the world. Her experiences and insight can be helpful to all who want to go into business for themselves.

Kathy's career before starting her business was varied and productive. She had been involved in management consulting, had been an executive officer in her family's personnel testing firm, and had worked on the governor's staff in Illinois. When her husband had to move to Arizona, she found that a void in her own life — work — and a void in the marketplace both needed filling.

Angered by the lack of stimulation available for her two gifted children in the public schools, Kathy was appointed by her district to head a committee to develop a program for gifted children. She began teaching seminars on the subject. Through her research she discovered how hard it was to find suitable materials for the program, and she decided to solve the problem by purchasing and marketing quality educational products.

In an effort to minimize overhead, Kathy stored her materials in a closet, mimeographed her order forms, and put her ping pong table and bathroom scales to good use in packaging her products and weighing the parcels. As her business began to grow, she added a shed and enclosed her carport for use as a combination storeroom and office.

Kathy's first mail-order catalog was sent to 3,500 parents and teachers who had attended her seminars. The response — 18 percent — was phenomenal in a business that considers 2 percent to be good. "I knew then I had found a tremendous need," she says. With a proven business behind her, she borrowed $250,000 and bought a building.

Today Kathy is the founder of five companies with 27 employees and sales in the $3.5 million range. In addition to mail order and publishing her own educational materials, she is involved in direct sales of products that teach thinking skills to parents and teachers, she provides management consulting and, in her latest venture, she profiles intellectual fitness for students and business people. Her nonprofit foundation — Think, Inc. — researches and develops ideas and educational programs related to thinking skills.

Kathy says she's in the business of teaching people to think. Her products are used in 30,000 schools ranging from pre-schools to universities in fifty states and fourteen foreign countries. Her goal, simply stated, is "to revolutionize the education of this country." She sees a continuing need for educational aids for young people. "If you can capture young minds and teach them problem-solving, it will stay with them for a lifetime," she explains.

In promoting problem-solving, one of the obstacles Kathy confronts is television. "What the kids see on TV is what goes on their Christmas list, and we fight Christmas lists all the time." With TV constantly promoting new fads for kids it's sometimes difficult to make them aware of her games, film strips, books and cassettes — all of which stimulate thinking skills, independence, creativity, communication, research, and investigation.

Kathy has some good advice for people entering the juvenile market, whether you choose to produce educational products, write for children, or retail some product:

- Use problem-solving techniques and approach your difficulties logically, but rely on your intuition, too. "The joy of being an entrepreneur is that you don't have to convince a board of directors [before taking action]. You've got to have the confidence to run with your instincts and believe in your abilities."

• Use advisers. In particular, hire an accountant as soon as you need one, but in the end, make your own decisions and set your own standards.

• Keep your goals and convictions in focus. "You have to be single-minded about some things, including your ability to break into the market. Decide on your goal, imagine yourself doing it and then go after it."

• Keep your overhead low. "I was profitable from the very start because I didn't rush out and buy new office furniture or build a fancy office when the orders started coming in."

• Keep a good dose of humor at your disposal, "or else you'll never make it."

Remember, in the juvenile market you're not really selling to the end user; you're selling to parents and teachers. Kids love a good idea, according to Kathy, TV or no TV. But parents and teachers care about packaging, so a successful entrepreneur will keep that in mind — without sacrificing the quality of the product.

ILLUSTRATION

While writers may question whether one picture is,

indeed, worth a thousand words, few will deny that the appearance of a book is important. For little people who can't read, this is especially true. A book's illustrations, cover and overall design promote the author's theme and can have a huge impact on sales.

As publishing houses tighten their belts, they continually look for ways to make their books more marketable. Attention-getting artwork is one of the approaches they're exploring, and that could mean freelance opportunities for you. According to *Writer's Market*, "In-house cost-cutting has included art staff reductions, thus creating more reliance on freelancers." Payment for artwork has risen or stayed the same, though, with fees varying from $10 to $4,000 for illustrations.

Besides books, today's 32,000 periodicals offer the most accessible market for freelance artists. Whereas a surprising number of book publishers want local artists in the New York or Boston area, magazine illustrators can more easily work by mail since most are not required to bring their portfolios in for the initial interview.

Book and magazine publishers have varying requirements and needs. Most want good composition and knowledgeable use of color for reproduction. Specific needs may include typography, lettering, book design, cover and text illustrations that include sketches, line drawings, cartoons, photography, watercolors, oils, washes, prints, technical drawings, or one- or two-color art.

Many publishers pay specific rates, but others will negotiate your fee. Some pay royalties, some buy one-time rights, and others want exclusive rights and will not return your original. Freelancers need to be familiar with the production process and must work within their alloted budgets, follow directions, meet deadlines and produce art that is up-to-date both stylistically and technically.

Some publishers want to see your portfolio during a personal interview but others are content with photocopied samples, slides, tearsheets and a resume or brochure. Some use freelancers exclusively but even those with art staffs may turn to freelancers when they have overflow work.

Whether you're investigating opportunities in magazines or books, check the publisher's most recent titles or issues at your library or bookstore. Just as writers do, artists may find it helpful to get together for constructive criticism of their work and to plan marketing strategies.

According to one successful illustrator and educator, a lot of art is being printed, and not much of it is especially good these days. "Artwork doesn't have to be great. It just has to fill a need," he points out. With juvenile publishing showing robust growth, competent, qualified juvenile illustrators may find a niche that's both fun and lucrative.

RETAIL TALES

Full-service bookstores and toy stores sell kids' books, of course, but small independently owned stores specializing in children's books have mushroomed in popularity in recent years. Ten years ago there were none, now there are about three hundred, according to the American Booksellers' Association (ABA).

Laurie Flores Children's Book and Music Center in Santa Monica, for example, has annual sales of more than $1 million; by comparison, 75 percent of ABA member stores sell less than $300,000 a year. Joan Flickes, owner of Adventures for Kids in Ventura, California, and a former children's librarian, began her store five years ago with a $30,000 investment. She sold $200,000 worth of books last year (with a 10 percent profit margin), and says sales have grown about 20 percent a year. Joel Fram opened his second Manhattan location and expects sales of $850,000 this year, up 15 percent from the year before.

Children's bookstore owners often rely on unusual marketing strategies to win customers, many of whom become regulars. Darlene Daniel, founder of Pages: Books for Children and Young Adults in Tarzana, California, hires teenagers who are avid readers and adults with teaching credentials to provide her customers with in-depth service. Joan Flickes speaks to groups of local parents and civic organizations about the importance of good books for children. Her store offers story hours, meetings with authors and illustrators, and facilities for parent group meetings as well.

As with clothes and toys, the way books are displayed can have a major impact on sales. It doesn't take a lot of room; Adventures for Kids uses only 900 square feet. It's a quiet, pleasant store with carpeting, open shelves and small sitting areas which invite children to browse. The shop's coziness makes shopping there a refreshing pleasure.

Freelance writing, illustrating, scriptwriting, educational aids, bookselling — the "write" stuff for children covers a lot of ground. It covers a lot of opportunities, too, for rewarding, challenging work. Barbara Steiner sums up her involvement in the field this way: "To me, it's a challenge being my own boss. And to me, it's a very creative way to work. The joy of it is that writing taxes my creativity plus I can do what I really enjoy and still be paid for it."

Chapter 9
A Mixed Bag
Of Other Opportunities

Anyone who's ever had a child, even one who was borrowed for an hour, knows at least one thing: Parents need help . . . all the help they can get.

You can provide that help in a variety of ways, and, in the process, set yourself up in business. For example,

- A 21-year-old economics major who juggles as a hobby earns $30 an hour as a clown at children's parties.

- A mother in New York City creates theme parties for children for a fee of $75 — plus all expenses.

- A woman in Colorado finds qualified nannies to provide in-home child care, and charges a placement fee of up to $350.

• A magician in Massachusetts earns up to $200 for 40-minute performances at parties.

Services for children run from the basic, bare essentials (such as diaper services) to indulgences (such as services that videotape graduations). Shopping help, nursery decorating services, toy repair, providing an escort — what you can offer to kids and their parents is limited only by your imagination.

Are you an artist? A writer? A compulsive shopper? An obsessive organizer? Whatever your skill and interest, you can market it if you're willing to commit your time and energy to getting your name out and to providing quality work.

SOME OPPORTUNITIES TO CONSIDER

Party Service

Children's parties are big business. One way to go to work in this field is to offer complete party planning to busy parents.

"Many parents would jump at the chance to have a professional party planner take over all the details of their children's birthday parties," say two self-employment experts. Mad Hatters, near Boston, produces parties based on themes popular with children — like clowns, dinosaurs, or favorite books. They decorate the house, organize games and crafts projects and provide favors and cake — all for a fee of $150 for a two-hour party with ten to fifteen guests. Creative Capers, also in Boston, charges anywhere from $125 to $500 for everything (from invitations to cleanup).

Birthdaybakers, Partymakers, run by Linda Kaye in New York City, is a bit more specialized. The business began when Linda asked a caterer friend to teach the guests at her daughter's sixth birthday party to bake a cake. The kids had so much fun she decided she had stumbled across a great idea and turned it into a business.

Linda arrives at the child's home with utensils and makings for a decorated birthday cake and a chef's hat and apron for the birthday child. If the parents would prefer to have the party away from their home, she charges $100 for use of two floors which she leases in an Upper East Side building and has furnished with a complete kitchen and work tables. Linda sends the parents invitations to address and mail, and provides diplomas and name tags for the guests. Additional chefs hats and aprons may be ordered for an extra charge.

Another way to go into the party business is to offer entertainment — such as puppet shows or magic shows — at children's parties. You might follow the example of Boston's Madame Nose, who plays the violin, juggles and tells stories and then makes balloon animals. Cheezo of Boston brings along a robot and charges from $50 to $75 and hour. Other clowns specialize in making up the children as clowns.

According to *Boston Magazine*, "Storytelling, the oldest and simplest of the theater arts, is enjoying a revival at the moment." The magazine lists six storytellers in the metropolitan area, one of whom charges

$100 per party. Some of the storytellers combine their art with music, dance, and a great deal of audience participation.

If you decide to go into the party business, consider these tips:

- Plan every minute and include some extra activities. Include both quiet and active games, but limit the time to about two hours.

- Think of a good way to get the party going. A crafts project is one suggestion, since it will involve even the shyest child.

- Seek out original party favors. They don't have to be expensive, but they shouldn't be junk either. Popular favors these days include inexpensive flashlights, stickers, small notebooks, colorful pens and pencils.

- If prizes are given out, be sure everyone gets something.

- End the party by giving out the favors. You can even give them on the condition that the kids open them at home, to ease the sorrow of parting. Nobody wants to end a good party; this is one way to motivate the guests to leave.

Entertainment Broker

If your primary talent is organization and you enjoy working with kids, a mini-talent agency might be the idea for you.

You can accumulate a "stable" of talent — jugglers, mimes, clowns, puppeteers, magicians, balloon sculptors — and book them for parties. Set a specific wage your entertainers will receive per party — and set your fee to the parents high enough so that you make a reasonable profit. One juggler who became an entertainment broker paid her clowns $20 for an hour of clowning and paid herself $10 more per hour for her time and effort.

When you audition your entertainers, try to learn as much as possible about the different skills they have. Find out how they'd react to different situations — kids spilling grape juice on a white carpet, kids fighting, kids being scared of a clown face, kids getting hurt. Teach them how to react in an emergency. Warn them that they'll be working crazy hours — mainly evenings and weekends.

According to a manual put out by the Harvard Entrepreneur Society, this type of entertainment brokering involves "finding clowns who want to work, arranging engagements for them, and laughing all the way to the bank." The guide continues, "A business like this has the potential to grow into a fairly good-sized operation. We feel this is an excellent kind of business for an entrepreneur who wants to proceed a step at a time."

Nanny Service

Karen Parker had an idea one snowy afternoon

after she got laid off from her job in the energy field. "It occurred to me that the biggest complaint of my friends with children is the difficulty of finding child care." Parker, who has no children of her own, decided to start a nanny service.

It took her about six months to get "Enchanted Nannies" off the ground, and the business has paid its own way since its inception.

"Working parents today have a real need to feel secure about their children while they're at their jobs. Plus, they feel guilty about leaving the children. Having a nanny allows them to come home to a clean house and children who are happy to see them. It gives them extra quality time with their family," she says.

Finding qualified nannies is her biggest problem. Parker requires three personal references, four or more professional references, a five-page application form, and a two-hour interview. Applicants must be fingerprinted and take classes in cardiopulmonary resusitation (CPR) and first aid, be at least 21 years old and have an educational or practical background in child care. The applicants Parker looks for are mature, positive and motivated people who like themselves and "don't need to be prodded."

Through the application and interview process, she hopes to discover how the prospective nanny will respond to irritating situations, emergencies and daily events in the lives of children. She *is* highly selective about whom she hires: "I can interview forty people in two weeks and only hire four or five," she says.

Even so, mistakes will be made. One nanny Parker

hired telephoned to tell the parent to come home when she discovered that one of the children had pink eye — and then she left. "I was livid," Parker recalled.

Most of the nannies work for single-parent families or families in which both parents work. It's not unusual for out-of-town visitors to call requesting a nanny to come to their hotel. Nannies also stay with children whose parents just want some time together, whether for an evening or a full-blown vacation.

Parker charges a placement fee of up to $350, which works much like a deposit, plus the nanny's hourly fee of $4. For heavy housework, the rate is higher, and for vacations the charge is $65 for a 24-hour period.

The nannies are not merely baby-sitters. They take their charges on trips to the library and the zoo, entertain them, and teach them, using a library of educational materials Parker has gathered together. The children range in age from four weeks to thirteen years.

Most of the nannies are either older women whose children are grown or college students who have taken early childhood development courses and work part time. Parker also hires graduates in education who haven't yet gotten jobs as teachers. "It's too bad for them, but it's great for me," she says.

Logistics are a big part of Parker's days. Not only does she find nannies and match them up with clients, she also arranges interviews so that the clients can choose between three or four different nannies.

Parker enthusiastically recommends starting such a business. Nannies are experiencing a rebirth of popularity in this country. "Everybody in their thirties is having children now. There's a definite move to this kind of child care because parents feel so secure knowing their child is in the home.''

And it's financially worthwhile: "It costs next to nothing,'' says Parker, who works out of her home. "You definitely can set up, maintain yourself and make a decent living.''

Diaper Service

They may not be glamorous, but diaper services can be profitable. In many areas of the country, and particularly the less populous counties, there is no competition at all. Even where services currently exist, you may be able to beat the competition by offering personalized service at a more economical rate.

All you need to start is a heavy-duty washer and dryer, some new, covered plastic garbage cans or hampers, a vehicle for deliveries and a ton of diapers. You'll need to buy your diapers, soap, and other supplies as cheaply as possible, so ask around to find a wholesale supplier.

In your advertising you can stress that parents will reduce the chance of diaper rash by using your service. By providing repeated washings, hotter water and mild detergent you can ensure cleaner, softer diapers.

Tout your service as the perfect gift for new parents. In fact, you may want to promote your new business by offering a week's service free to all the babies born during your first week of business.

Custom Cards

Unlike royalty, whose births traditionally are announced by cannon fire, the rest of us turn to calligraphers and artists for custom-designed birth announcements. Bar Mitzvah, confirmation, party, and graduation invitations or annoucements offer additional opportunities for providing personalized cards.

To set yourself up in the personalized card business, design a flier that explains your service with the same flair, clarity, and visual impact that your cards will have. Ask shop owners to help you drum up business in return for a small referral fee, or better yet, in exchange for some personalized cards for them.

Success will depend entirely on your creativity, so consider all possibilities. In birth announcements, for example, you may want to incorporate photographs of the baby, original poetry, humor, or original art. Of course, you'll include the baby's name and date of birth, along with the parent's names. The baby's weight, height, and place of birth are often mentioned, as well.

When the orders start rolling in, be sure to include your name (and phone number if you can do so unobtrusively and tastefully) on the back of the cards or announcements.

Photography Service

"Of all the businesses involving children, photography is one of the surest money-makers," say self-employment experts Vino Bennett and Cricket Clagett.

From films or photographs of the birth to videotaping the child's high school graduation, you can offer proud parents the most vivid reminder possible of the milestones of their child's life.

You could contract your services through department stores, schools, churches, clubs, teams, child care centers — even high school yearbooks are a possibility. You might advertise that you shoot Christmas card photos, family or individual portraits, photos for mugs or t-shirts. You could also specialize in blowing up photos into posters or wall murals.

Escort Service

The increase in kidnappings and disappearing children means that parents want — and need — to know that their kids are in good hands. It's unfortunate that we have to be so concerned with safety today, but that concern could mean business for you.

You could start a business driving kids to and from weekend matinees or high school football games and dances. Weekly trips could be scheduled to the local ice skating rink in winter and the pool in summer.

You'll need a van, adequate insurance and, possibly, special licensing to operate such a service.

GETTING STARTED

Once you've settled on an idea your first step is to investigate every service in your town which is similar to your idea. Talk to retailers, teachers, parents, and others who serve the juvenile market. What do they think about your idea? Who do they know who offers anything even remotely similar to your idea? How did they get started? What legal or marketing obstacles did they confront? Are they busy? What mistakes did they make?

Next, talk to an accountant to help you set up your records, estimate your expenses and figure out what to charge. Other people offering similar services — and parents — can also help you decide on a realistic fee.

MARKETING

Once you know what you want to do, how you're going to do it and how much you'll charge for it, the next step is to get the word out.

A good way to get started might be to have a logo designed by a graphic artist. Used on all advertising, your statements, stationery, and business cards, a logo presents a consistent, professional image of your business to the public. It indicates that you're serious about what you do and that you care about how you are perceived.

Next you'll want to have fliers printed up with your logo and all pertinent information about your services. Use eye-catching graphics and interest-grabbing language to explain what you do, how your services can benefit children and/or adults, and how people can get in touch with you. It's a good idea to invest in an answering service or an answering machine so you don't miss the calls when they start coming in.

Since you're offering a service of interest to families, distribute your fliers where they'll do the most good — meetings for parents at schools, women's clubs, church and civic group meetings, city recreation department, or pool, maternity, or children's shops.

Talk to retail store owners and others in the children's market and ask them how effective newspaper or radio advertising has been for them. If one or the other seems to be an effective medium in your town, give it a try. Consider offering a first-time discount in the beginning — it may help you round up those first, crucial customers. Once you've established yourself with a few customers, word of the quality of your service will spread.

Visit your local newspaper editor and, if possible, offer him or her a free demonstration or sample of what you do. Leave a typed sheet with the essential facts about your service — your background, what you do, how you got the idea, why it's unique in your town, your experience, and — most important — how people can reach you. In other words, do everything you can to make it easy and desirable for a story to be written about you.

In Conclusion

As more and more mothers enter the workforce, as more two-family kids are involved in custody arrangements following divorces, the demand for services that provide help to busy parents will continue to grow. If you take pleasure in making people's lives easier, such a business could be a rewarding career for you.

Chapter 10
Running a Business:
Getting Started in the Race

"You've gotta be nuts."
— Don Koplen

The words above — by an entrepreneur who has started several businesses of his own, has lectured to university business classes and now works as a consultant to other small business owners — were echoed by every one of the several dozen people interviewed for this book. And, like the others, Koplen was quick to add, "But I sure wouldn't want to work for anybody else!"

The amount of time, research, headaches, anxiety, and money you'll invest in launching your business will undoubtedly be greater than you imagine, but the rewards will also be greater. For one thing, the juvenile market generously spawns fortunes for the right ideas marketed the right way at the right time. Then too, owning your own business will reward you with a tremendous amount of satisfaction, one that many people equate with having a child. You never imagined the drain of sleepless nights, the agony of a temper tantrum during dinner at your favorite restaurant, the despair over a prolonged fever. On the other hand, neither did you dream of the joy from an unasked-for hug, the pleasure of sharing your favorite book, the pride from watching a young mind develop independence and responsibility. You wouldn't trade those experiences for anything, right?

Running a business can provide similar pleasures. As a small business owner, you can know the satisfaction of offering a product or service that your customers really want, take pride in doing a job the way it should be done, and experience the thrill of watching your enterprise grow. It's yours! You thought of it. You took the risks. You created it. You asked the right questions and came up with the right answers.

PERSONAL ACCOUNTING

What are your personal assets and liabilities?

Do you really believe in your idea? "Not all the people you talk to are going to think your idea is so great," Koplen says. "The main thing you can bring to a new business is that you believe in yourself and you know your idea is really going to work" — despite the doomsayers.

Most entrepreneurs either have a strong streak of independence or feel that their idea has potential for a higher return than anything else they can do. "You're gambling that you'll get a better return from this idea you love so much, and your gamble is as much emotional as it is financial," Koplen continues.

Successful entrepreneurs, according to the experts, are self-confident, goal-oriented, thick-skinned self-starters. They are responsible, decisive, persevering, optimistic, and competitive. You may be strong in some areas and weaker in others, but that's to be expected. Just the fact that you've come up with an idea you believe in and are committed to says a great deal about your drive, creativity, and optimism. You can take classes in assertiveness to build your self-esteem and communication skills if necessary. Business management classes can help hone your organizational abilities and may awaken a latent competitiveness you didn't realize was part of your personality. And, when push comes to shove, you can hire people with interests or skills that you lack.

Try to be objective about what you can best contribute to your business and concentrate your energy on that. Examine your immediate finances, too. You may want your lawyer to help you protect your assets from possible losses.

Are you prepared for more work than you ever imagined? "If you think you can do it only from eight to five, don't do it," Koplen advises. The first few months — even years — of owning your own business will require total dedication and all-out effort.

THE RIGHT QUESTIONS

What follows is a general guide to the fine art of asking questions. It's only a beginning. By asking the right questions, though, you'll guide yourself down the path toward information which is crucial for the success of your business.

Your first step is to sit down with pen in hand and actually write out your business concept. Be specific. Be very clear about what you want to do. Next you'll need to survey the market to find out exactly how your concept can fit in and be competitive.

Remember that it's impossible to ask too many questions. Especially for a woman new to the world of business, it can be hard to assert yourself enough to take up someone else's time in order to ask your questions. People love to talk, though, especially when they can see that you're sincerely interested in what they have to say. Candidly tell them that you want to pick their brains for fifteen minutes about their experiences. Chances are they'll be flattered, and they'll end up giving you a lot more time than that. They'll tell you when they need to get back to work, so don't worry about impinging on their busy schedules. Just keep asking questions.

Talk to competitors, suppliers, and trade groups. Many trade groups offer courses that can help you become familiar with specialized aspects of the industry. They may be able to give advice about what is selling, and trade group functions can be a great place to make valuable contacts.

Is there a local, state or national organization that

addresses your concerns as a business person or as someone involved with kids? Join it. Talk to your local Chamber of Commerce, too.

You need to find out everything you possibly can about how your product or service can be successful in the market. Journalists rely on "five Ws and an H" to get them through interviews. The same questions apply to you, too, in your initial person-to-person research.

WHAT: What, exactly, is it that you're going to be selling? What are the features and benefits of your product or service? What advantages exist for the consumer? What potential drawbacks, if any, can you see with your product or service?

WHO: Who is going to buy your product or service? Marketing professionals speak of the importance of knowing customer demographics and psychographics. "Demographics" relate to facts such as where your customers live, their age, race, income levels, educational levels and so forth. "Psychographics" are more subjective factors that have to do with self-image and related psychological characteristics. They can be just as important as demographics in helping you to understand what motivates potential customers to buy — or not buy — from you. One way to find out this kind of information is to conduct a simplified survey of likely customers.

Who is going to help you make or sell your idea? When hiring advisers (such as a lawyer or accountant) or employees, question them closely. You deserve nothing less than the best, so you must make sure that's what you get. Follow your instincts as well as your logic in choosing the people you work with. And if you're going to make your business a partnership, be doubly careful. Partnerships, like marriages, can be easier to form than to dissolve.

Who else has done what you want to do? What have their experiences been? What advice do they have for you? If those in similar businesses are reluctant to talk to you, you might try going to another town where you won't be a potential competitor. Ask those in similar businesses what they did right — and wrong — when they started their business. If they could do it over again, what would they do differently? If possible, lay the groundwork for a long-term relationship with those who give you helpful advice. It may seem like you have all the answers you need, but tomorrow will bring a new set of questions.

WHERE: Where will you set up your office or work space? How much room do you need? Where's the most economical, practical location for you? Where will you market you goods or services?

WHEN: When can you realistically expect to launch your business? How many hours a week will it require — both now, in the planning and research stage — and later, when it's up and running? Scheduling is crucial to your success and sanity. Sit down and devise a workable plan for the days, weeks, and months ahead. You're going to be busier than you can imagine soon, so be sure to set aside some time for yourself and your family, too.

WHY: What is your underlying motivation for starting this business? This is more important than it may seem. As publisher Kathy Kolbe put it, you probably will not succeed if you're only after fortune or fame. If you genuinely love kids and really, truly believe in your idea, however, you've got what it takes to succeed and make it through all the long days and nights ahead of you.

HOW: Finally, how are you going to pull it off? How much will your equipment cost? Where can you buy it or lease it? Where will you buy your supplies? You need details: prices, availability, shipping, storage, procedures, and time frames. Break your idea down into manageable chunks and then plan your way through the maze — step by step, one step at a time. Develop production plans, financial plans, marketing plans, staffing plans. Have some contingency plans in mind, too. What will you do if your business is an instant, smashing success? What will you do if it's *not*?

. . . AND MORE QUESTIONS

You'll need to find out about any legal requirements that affect you, and that means talking to officials in your city or county. They can tell you about zoning, health, and safety regulations, and any permits you'll be required to have. Registering your business name may or may not be required where you live, but it's a good idea to register it anyway, because that can prevent someone else from using the same name.

A good accountant can help you set up your books and show you how to keep track of your expenses for tax purposes. Keeping accurate business records is a time-consuming but essential chore for any successful business.

Local bankers can tell you what kind of help they're willing to extend to a business such as yours. Ask them to explain their policies on loans, collateral, balance requirements, interest, co-signers, overdrafts, and personal guarantees for debts.

A lawyer can explain the advantages and disadvantages of the various ways you can organize your business. Should you be a sole proprietor? Should you form a partnership, or a limited partnership? What about incorporating?

Shop around for a qualified, reputable insurance broker who handles other small business clients like you. Insist that he or she visit your business and specify recommendations in clear language. Read and understand the policy, and look for loopholes. Establish the habit of reviewing your policy yearly and of getting bids from other brokers every few years.

If any of these professionals suddenly begin speaking a language you don't understand, ask them to explain themselves in English. Question them until what they're saying makes sense. Don't be shy! You're not the first person who's ever been confused by a legal contract or an insurance policy.

Shop around for suppliers, too. Find several you can depend on; it's unwise to limit yourself to one. Work at developing good, solid relationships with them because suppliers can often make the difference between success and failure — especially when a business is just getting off the ground.

Help From the Federal Government

In the early stages of your planning you should contact the Small Business Administration. Established specifically to help people like you, the SBA offers a wealth of valuable information. Its staff can help you plan your procedures and figure out profit-and-loss projections to help you anticipate your expenditures. They can also send you some of the more than two hundred free or low-cost booklets they publish on topics like record-keeping, tax reporting, insurance — you name it. They'll help you understand the requirements of other agencies in the bureaucracy. They can provide consulting, quick information, research, publicity advice — and in some cases, money and help with training employees.

Other government agencies offer assistance, too. The post office can teach you about sending your mailings at the most economical rate. The Library of Congress National Referral Center has thousands of specialists throughout the country, and your local Federal Information Center offers help, as well. The Bureau of Census Data Users' Service can tell you about population patterns, business sales, family income, and retail statistics. The Department of Commerce publishes information for businesses and helps promote business development.

SETTING UP HOUSE

It's time to get down to business, so to speak. To

begin with, you'll need to put together a profit-and-loss statement which projects your expenses and income for at least one year. Also known as an operating statement or income statement, your "P & L" will focus on the costs of goods and services needed to produce your revenues, including rent, materials, wages, taxes, advertising, licenses, etc.

"Examine all your expenses and multiply the costs by two. Decrease your income expectations by 50 percent, and if it still works, do it," Koplen advises. "It always costs more, takes more time, and is more difficult than you think."

Now begin your housekeeping. Open a checking account in your business name and use it only for business expenses. If you want to take money out, write yourself a check, but avoid writing business checks for personal expenses (it makes bookkeeping unnecessarily complicated). Use your new checks to take out whatever licenses and permits you need.

Figure out exactly what you'll do with the receipts and bills that will come in faster than you can believe. "Decide how you're going to keep them, even if it's only a shoe box that you hand to your accountant," advises Koplen. You should keep receipts and records from the moment you start investigating your idea. Your records will detail purchases, sales, inventory, depreciation, payroll, credit, collections, personnel, and expenses. Don't despair — it's not terribly complicated and a basic bookkeeping course can teach you all you need to know.

In the beginning, you'll need to keep your overhead

as low as possible. Kathy Kolbe says, "Don't invest more in your new business than you can afford to lose." That may mean working at home, taking over the garage or the ping pong table, as she did. It may mean only visiting an accountant once at first and then keeping track of your expenses and tax records yourself. And it certainly means *not* planning on using your first profits for a trip to the Bahamas. "Wait awhile to see your cash-flow pattern," Kolbe advises. "Don't expect immediate success. Plan for it to take at least two years before your business makes a profit." Unless you have the capital or an independent source of income, start small and build your business gradually, probably while you hold down another job. Then, when it's going well and you know it can support you, quit your job.

There are three things you'll need to consider if you decide not to start your business in your home: location, location, location. For certain types of businesses (particularly retail shops) having the right location is absolutely essential. How much you can afford is one criteria, of course, but there are others as well. Do you need to be in a high-traffic area that will attract customers, in an established shopping area, for example, or near a popular mall? Do you need parking for your customers? If you're not opening a store you still may need to consider access for shipping and receiving, or storage for your materials. And don't forget about zoning regulations.

Once you've found an available space in the right location, study the lease with a critical eye. Know who's responsible for paying for utilities and water, for alterations, additions, fixtures; who's responsible for your personal property in case of damage from leaky pipes, negligence of other tenants or fire; what happens if you suddenly decide to sublease some space or if you default on your payments. To be safe, have an attorney look it over before you sign. Lease only as much as you really need and use it to its fullest potential.

Once you're underway, don't be so in love with your product that you aren't willing to make changes, Margaret Hansson advises. Finding a better-made part may affect your design. A more reliable supplier may mean a different color or more durable fabrics. Be responsive to market feedback and the lessons of experience. "The product doesn't know you own it," Hansson comments. In her experience, customer demand meant an expanded line of baby carriers — and her initial success.

"Remain skeptical," Hansson says. And be flexible. "If it doesn't succeed wildly, bring in another product. A single product might not make it, but an expanded line might," she adds.

Cultivate your suppliers, both the manufacturers and their sales reps. They'll teach you about quality, about trends — and about what your competition is up to. Pay them on time, at least part of what you owe them, and always treat them courteously, no matter how busy you are when they pop in.

The Importance of Promotion

Promotion can make or break your business. Don't

believe that stuff about the world beating a path to your door if you build a better mousetrap. You may have the greatest product since diapers, but somehow you still have to get the word out and be convincing.

Your local media sales reps will help you place your ads, but they're clearly not unbiased. You may want to hire a professional, at least once, to help with your ad designs and show you how to manage an effective promotion.

The ad copy, design, color, and logo — even the name of your company — are tools you can use to fix yourself clearly in your customers' minds. Your ads should stress what's different about your products or services to give you an edge over the competition. They should catch your customers' attention by showing them how you're distinctive and how you can best meet their needs.

Promotion includes all types of paid advertising, but it goes far beyond just placing an occasional ad in your local paper. The brochures you hand out, the radio and TV interviews you succeed in lining up, your business listing in the phone book — even the discounts and free classes you offer in your shop are part of your overall promotional effort.

In fact, it's probably smart not to rely on paid ads at first, except perhaps for special events. Try to outsmart your competition rather than outspend them. Work hard at getting free publicity and give the kind of personalized service that results in word-of-mouth advertising. Keep track of where your customers heard about you and repeat what works — again and again.

If you're manufacturing a specialty item like Al and Lois Hough's Janesville Coaster Wagon, you may decide to market regionally or nationally rather than locally. Would ads in specialized magazines work for you? Display ads can cost a small fortune; like Dale Prohaska, you may find it makes more sense to test the market with a small classified ad for some months.

Whatever marketing approach you decide upon, remember that, over the long run, the amount of quality and care you can build into your business will make all the difference. What this boils down to is the nitty-gritty of how often you vacuum your shop, how pleasant you sound on the phone, how promptly you pay your bills and fill your orders. Your goal, always, is to generate sales. Being conscientious is a means to that end because pleased customers will return — and so will their friends.

In the juvenile market, the possibilities for being rewarded for your creativity are unlimited. It's a market that's always open to new ideas and that rewards the best of those ideas bountifully. Every day will be different for you — the problems you confront, the people you meet, the parents or kids who are thrilled with what you give them.

In the end, you'll thrive as your business does. In your heart, you'll know that you did it. Your idea, your effort, your determination, your ingenuity, and hard work will mean satisfaction and financial success. Business is one of the last frontiers for individual achievement and exploration, and the juvenile market offers unique paths to creativity, fun and income.

Appendix
Additional Resources

Organizations

New Careers Center, P.O. Box 297, Boulder, CO 80306 (mail-order source for books, tapes and other materials on all aspects of self-employment and career change — send name and address for catalog/newsletter)

Children's Foundation, 1420 New York Ave., NW No. 80, Washington, D.C. 20005 (347-3300. (Headquarters for National Family Day Care Advocacy Project)

Juvenile Products Manufacturing Association, 66 E. Main St., Moorestown, NJ 08057 (609) 234-9156

National Association of Women Business Owners, 500 N. Michigan Ave., Suite 1400, Chicago, IL 60611 (312) 661-1700

Small Business Administration, Washington, D.C. 20416

Toys N Things Press, division of Child Caring, Inc., 906 N. Dale St., St. Paul, Minn. 55103 (612) 488-7284. A nonprofit agency offering training programs, support services and resources for family day-care providers, foster parents, nursery and day-care center staff, trainers and parents. Its catalogue includes business ideas, a calendar-record keeper, ideas for working with parents and help with preparing tax returns.

National Association for the Education of Young Children, 1834 Connecticut Ave., N.W. Washington, D.C. 20009 (800) 424-2460

Periodicals

Small World, Earn Shaw Publishing, Inc., 393 7th Ave., New York, NY 10001

Juvenile Merchandising, Columbia Communications, Inc., 370 Lexington Ave., New York, NY 10011

Sew Business, 1271 Avenue of the Americas, New York, NY 10020

Books

(Classes)
Teaching Instrumental Music George Duerksen. D.C.

Music Educators' National Conference, 1972.

Learning to Teach Art, Robert Paston. Lincoln, NB: Professional Educators: 1973.

Teaching Art Basics, Roy Sparkes. Cincinnati: Watson-Guptill, 1973.

How to Teach Foreign Languages Effectively, Theodore Huebener, NY: New York University Press, 1976.

Cooking Adventures for Kids, Sharon Calwallader. Boston: Houghton Mifflin Co., 1974.

Kids are Natural Cooks, Parent's Nursery School. Boston: Houghton Mifflin Co., 1974.

Activities Handbook for Teachers of Young Children, Doreen Croft and Robert Hess. Boston: Houghton Mifflin Co., 1972.

(Child Care)
A House Full of Kids, Karen Murphy. Boston: Beacon Press, 1984.

Family Day Care, Squibb. The Harvard Common Press.

Spoonful of Lovin': A Manual for Day Care Providers. Agency for Instructional Television.

Business Ideas for Family Day Care Providers. Toys N Things Press.

Guide for Family Day Care. E.I.D. Associates.

Cooking for the 1-9 Year Old. Coop. Ext. Services, Colorado State University, Fort Collins, Colorado.

Mother's Almanac, Marguerite Kelly and Elias Parsons. New York: Doubleday, 1975.

(Clothing)
Sewing Children's Clothes: A Golden Hands Pattern Book. NY: Random House, 1973.

Children's Wear Design, Hilda Jaffe. NY: Fairchild 1972.

Making Children's Clothes, Joan Moloney. NY: Drake Publishers, 1970.

From Rags to Riches: Success in Apparel Retailing, Marvin E. Segal. Wiley, 1982.

The Children's Exchange Operations Manual, Karen Lynch. 33 Inn Street Mall, Newburyport, MA 01950

(Toys)
Kids'-Play, Bank Street College. Ballantine, 1984.

Making Costume Dolls, Jean Greenhowe. NY: Watson-Guptill, 1973.

Costume Dolls and How to Make Them, Winifred

Craven. Plainfiled, NJ: Textile Book Service, 1968.

How to Make Dolls' Houses, Audrey Johnson. Newton Center, Mass: Branford, 1972.

Furnishing Dolls' Houses, Audrey Johnson. Newtown Center, Mass: Branford, 1972.

(Camps)
Recreation Program Guide: Organizing Activities for School, Camp, Park, Playground for Children's Club, Jean Kujoth. Metuchen, NJ: Scarecrow Press, 1972.

Recreation Today: Program Planning and Leadership, Richard Kraus. NY: Appleton-Century-Crofts, 1977.

Nature Recreation: Group Guidance for the Out-of-Doors, William Venal. Gloucester, Mass: Peter Smith.

(Accessories)
How to Make Children's Furniture and Play Equipment, Mario Fabbro. NY: McGraw Hill, 1975.

Making Children's Furniture and Play Structures, Bruce Palmer. NY: Workman, 1974.

How to Make Your Own Greeting Cards, John Carlis. Cincinnati: Watson-Guptill, 1968.

Banners and Hangings: Design and Construction, Norman Laliberte and Sterling McIlhandy. NY: Van Nostrad, 1966.

Mobiles: A Practical Guide for Beginners, Peter Mytton-Davies. NY: International Publications, 1971.

(Writing)
The Writer's Market, P.J. Schemenaur, ed. Cinncinnati: Writer's Digest Books, annual.

The Complete Guide to Writing Non-Fiction, Glen Evans, editor. NY: American Society of Journalists and Authors, 1983.

(Services)
Betty Crocker's Parties for Children, Louis Freeman, ed. Racine, WI: Western Publishing, 1964.

You Can be a Puppeteer, Carolyn London. Chicago: Moody Press, 1972.

How to Successfully Start and Operate a Doll Hospital, Edle Torngren. Riverdale, MD: Hobby House Press, 1969.

Professional Magic for Amateurs, Walter Gibson. NY: Peter Smith, 1974.

How I Photograph Children, Suzanne Szasz. NY: American Photographic Book Publishing, 1973.

Handbook for Storytellers, Caroline Feller Bauer. American Library Association, 1977.

38 Ways to Amuse a Child, June Johnson. New York: MacMillan, 1970.

(Business, general)
How to Become Financially Successful by Owning Your Own Business, Albert J. Lowry. NY: Simon and Schuster, 1981.

Opening Your Own Retail Store, Lyn Taetzsch. Chicago: Contemporary Books, Inc., 1977.

How to Start Your Own Craft Business, Lyn Taetzsch and Herb Genfan. NY: Watson-Guptill Publications, 1974.